DOWN UNDER MILK WOOD

Andrew Sinclair

This edition published in 2014 by Timon Films Limited,
Flat 20, Millennium House, 132 Grosvenor Road, London SW1V 3JY

ISBN 978-0-9576885-1-3

Printed in Great Britain and distributed by Witley Press Ltd,
24-26 Greevegate, Hunstanton, PE36 6AD
Email: bookshop@witleypress.co.uk
Website: www.witleypress.co.uk

Distribution and sales: Reel Solutions, Dean Clough,
Halifax HX3 5AX
Website: www.reelsolutions.co.uk

www.undermilkwoodfilm.com

UNDER MILK WOOD

CAST LIST

1st Voice	RICHARD BURTON
Rosie Probert	ELIZABETH TAYLOR
Captain Cat	PETER O'TOOLE
Myfanwy Price	GLYNIS JOHNS
Mrs Pugh	VIVIEN MERCHANT
Mrs Ogmore-Pritchard	SIAN PHILLIPS
Mog Edwards	VICTOR SPINETTI
2nd Voice	RYAN DAVIES
Gossamer Beynon	ANGHARAD REES
Nogood Boyo	DAVID JASON
Mr Waldo	RAY SMITH
Sinbad Sailors	MICHAEL FORREST
Polly Garter	ANN BEACH
Mr Cherry Owen	GLYN EDWARDS
Mrs Cherry Owen	BRIDGET TURNER
Mr Pugh	TALFRYN THOMAS
Mr Willy Nilly	WIM WYLTON
Mrs Willy Nilly	BRONWEN WILLIAMS
Lily Smalls	MEG WYNN OWEN
Butcher Beynon	HUBERT REES
Mrs Beynon	MARY JONES
The Rev Eli Jenkins	AUBREY RICHARDS
Evans The Death	MARK JONES
Mr Ogmore	DILLWYN OWEN

CAST LIST (continued)

Mr Pritchard	RICHARD DAVIES
Lord Cut Glass	DAVYDD HAVARD
Utah Watkins	DAVID DAVIES
Mrs Utah Watkins	MAUDIE EDWARDS
Ocky Milkman	GRIFFITH DAVIES
Bessie Bighead	PEGGY ANN CLIFFORD
Dai Bread	DUDLEY JONES
Norma Jane	PAT KAVANAGH
Mrs Dai Bread One	DOROTHEA PHILLIPS
Mrs Dai Bread Two	RUTH MADOC
PC Attila Rees	DAVYD HARRIES
Mary Ann Sailors	RACHEL THOMAS
Waldo Wife One	ANDREE GAYDON
Second Woman & Waldo Wife Two	EIRA GRIFFITHS
First Neighbour & Waldo Wife Three	MARGARET COURTENAY
First Woman & Waldo Wife Four	RHODA LEWIS
Waldo Wife Five	PAMELA MILES
Jack Black	JOHN REES
Mrs Rose Cottage	JILL BRITTON
Mae Rose Cottage	SUSAN PENHALIGON
Inspector	EDMOND THOMAS
Organ Morgan	RICHARD PARRY
Mrs Organ Morgan	DILYS PRICE
Gwennie	OLWEN REES
Mother	IRIS JONES
1st Fisherman	GORDON STYLES
2nd Fisherman	BRIAN OSBOURNE

CAST LIST (continued)

1st Drowned Sailor	SHANE SHELTON
2nd Drowned Sailor	PAUL GRIST
3rd Drowned Sailor	BRYN JONES
4th Drowned Sailor	JOHN RAINER
5th Drowned Sailor	BRYN WILLIAMS
Villager in Sailors Arms	ALDWYN FRANCIS
Villager in Sailors Arms	IFOR OWEN
Villager in Sailors Arms	DUDLEY OWEN
Woman Villager in Sailors Arms	GLADYS WYKEHAM-EDWARDS
Gomer Owen	IENAN RHYS WILLIAMS
Old Man	T.H. EVANS
Second Neighbour	GWYNETH OWEN
Third Neighbour	LUCY GRIFFITHS
Fourth Neighbour	ANGELA BRINKWORTH

TECHNICAL CREDITS

Producer	TIMON FILMS
Co-Producers:	JULES BUCK
	HUGH FRENCH
Director	ANDREW SINCLAIR
Screenwriter	ANDREW SINCLAIR
Associate Producer	JOHN COMFORT
Location Manager	LEE BOLAN
Assistant Director	DOMINIC FULFORD
Continuity Girl	ANN SKINNER
Casting Director	MIRIAM BRICKMAN
Director of Photography	BOB HUKE
Camera Operator	DENNIS LEWISTON
Sound Mixer	CYRIL COLLICK
Art Director	GEOFFREY TOZER
Music by	BRIAN GASCOIGNE
Construction Manager	FRED GUNNING
Editor	WILLY KEMPLEN
Wardrobe Mistress	DULCIE MIDWINTER
Wardrobe Master	ROY PONTING
Chief Make-Up Artist	ERIC ALLWRIGHT
Peter 0'Toole's Make-Up	CHARLES PARKER
Hairdresser	JOAN WHITE
Property Master	MICK LENNON
Property Mistress	JACQUEMINE
	CHARROTT-LODWIDGE

DYLAN AND I

There was one voice, who sang like the waking dawn to us in the early years of the 'fifties. As the owls, which were bearing the farm away, the words of Dylan Thomas carried our hopes and our dreams on brown wings somewhere beyond sense and halfway to heaven. There was really not much imagination or incitement in those doldrums of postwar time, and his wild words, so carefully wrought in the nightingales of verse, were our bards and minstrels. He was a funny curly fellow, too, beer-brightness and belly-laughter with his tales of Welsh innocents in the bad pubs of the city, and a regret for the lost wonder of the hills and the spinneys and the fields.

Roistering and raving, firing with vertigos like another Baudelaire, Dylan was for us a release and a delight, an earthy spirit. We were an inhibited generation of war children, rationed and deprived. Then Dylan deluged us with all the treasures of Myfanwy Price's general store, gobstoppers, jellybabies, hundreds and thousands for the mouth and the mind. When we heard his poems, we knew that there was much living to be gotten.

Dylan was the best speaker of himself, with his rich voice enjoying hugely what he had written. After him, Richard Burton and Emlyn Williams were the magic tongues of those incantations that seemed to haunt many of us, the more we heard them.

> There was a Saviour
> Rarer than radium
> Commoner than water, crueller than truth…

Dylan was not religious, yet he could not escape from God. He was a Swansea boy, who was the blessed bard for the Welsh valleys and seas and hills. He boozed his life away, because he found too many friends and parasites at the bar – dying of strangers. He discovered that the seven virtues were deadly, too. A creature of opposites, he could never put together his contrary nature and divided wants without the healing labour of his craft or sullen art. What drove him to his early dying was not writing enough poetry, the damned waste of it all.

> On no work of words now for three lean months in the bloody
> Belly of the rich year and the big purse of my body
> I bitterly take to task my poverty and craft…

Yet, prodigal as he was of his speech and his flesh and the hours of his days, Dylan was no Oscar Wilde, to devote his genius to his life, leaving only his talent for his art. His fine poems are enough to stock a memory, while his marvellous tales and plays about Wales create a comic nostalgia for a country, where most of us were never young. The quality of his prose is so hypnotic that it transports us to his childhood, while we are oblivious of our own. We were all at that Christmas over there with the fat uncles and the fierce aunts. Only the greater writers can make their remembrances more significant than our own. After listening to Dylan, I am more sure that I spent my boyhood in the Mumbles than in the wartime suburbs of Oxford and Port Meadow.

That offer of making his experience so universal turned Dylan into a people's poet. I would see *AND DEATH SHALL HAVE NO DOMINION* and *DO NOT GO GENTLE INTO THAT GOOD NIGHT* carved on many a tombstone near Aberystwyth and Caernarvon. When I was to make the film of *Under Milk Wood* and play it at Venice and in Madrid, I could see the common warm humanity of the pictures of village life, tickling and moving the audiences, who could only take in the music of the words without understanding them. They would laugh and weep, because Dylan's images of Llaregyb reminded them of the Sicily of Verga and the Spain of Lorca. A proud moment for me would be Dylan's widow Caitlin, saying at the London *première*: "That is exactly as Dylan would want to show it."

At Dylan's dying in New York with the quotation, "I've had eighteen straight whiskies, is that a record?", Caitlin had gone off her head. Maddened with grief and booze, on the liner home, she had been sent down to bunk with the sailors and play cards on the top of her dead husband's portable bier, before being summoned on high to the Captain's

Table. Then she had to take his embalmed body in a check suit with a red bow tie, contained in a glass-topped coffin back to Laugharne. When Wynford Vaughan Thomas saw the dressy corpse, he said, "Dylan wouldn't be seen dead in that." Evans the Death had driven his hearse down from Wales to collect the cargo from Portsmouth docks. Late for the funeral ceremony, a call was received from Cornwall. Evans was complaining. "I headed west," he said, "but nobody told me this bloody country was forked."

As a Trustee of the Thomas Estate, Wynford told me that the burial of Dylan was the usual sprint to pick off the flesh from the body of the genius. Standing at the graveside, he saw a pair of notorious literary ravens begin to sidle over the hill. He knew of a short cut through the village, and so he legged it to the Boathouse, just to discover the brace of scavengers stuffing a few manuscripts into their pockets.

Chasing them away and trying to lock up the Dylan doors and windows, he remembered another duty to the Thomas Estate, whatever it might be worth. Caitlin would be plastered at the wake in Brown's Hotel, and some smart agent would be getting the better of her for cash down for a few more schooners of booze. And so Wynford found her signing away on the back of an envelope the literary copyrights of her husband for a slim wad of tenners on the booth table. Wynford tore up the paper and bundled the chancer into a broom cupboard and wedged the door.

"And so," he told me with pride, "I preserved the Thomas estate."

In her *Leftover Life to Kill*, the bereaved Caitlin with her three children wrote that she could not believe Dylan was dead and gone:

> Dylan and dying, Dylan and dying, they don't go together; or is it that they were bound to go together; he said so often enough, but I did not heed him … Jesus, he even kept saying he would die before me; would never reach forty: and I would be a flighty widow dancing on his grave.

And he did die at thirty-nine years old. And because of my later film of *Under Milk Wood*, which located Dylan's fishing village of Llaregyb in Lower Fishguard, Wynford Vaughan Thomas would, as a local landowner, help to preserve that small haven, too. And so it was to happen – a time warp of a little harbour as a ship in a bottle for the marvel of future generations, a memorial to the greatest Welsh bard of his days.

In death as well as life, Dylan mixed comedy with tragedy. Richard Burton would tell me that Dylan had insisted on reciting to him the finest poem in the English language. It ran:

I AM
THOU ART
HE, SHE, IT IS
WE ARE
YOU ARE
THEY ARE

Dylan was the bard of our being. We were allies in what he wrote. When I later tried to catch his complexity in a biography, Caitlin would be kind about the lack of success of my writing: "You have picked the plums and touched the living quick of the Dylan situation with penetrating insight... What baffles me is from whence first did your passion and your understanding come?" I do not know, but I only know this. By Dylan's own words shall we know him, and perhaps ourselves, a little more, for better and worse.

Since I was young and easy under the apple boughs, I had wanted to write of Dylan the Bard, where the trail began in a time before time. So as he wrote in *Under Milk Wood*, I tried to begin at the beginning. Thomas Gray's ode on 'The Bard' had praised the names of Urien and Taliesin, who meant the 'bright and shining brow' of the spirit. As he sang:

I was instructor
To the whole Universe.
I shall be until the judgement
On the face of the earth.

After Taliesin in the Dark Ages, the bards of ancient Wales were either master poets patronised at the Welsh court or minstrels wandering from village to inn, telling their tales for bread and shelter.

As Widsith in the early English poem of the *Far Traveller,* they were heard as Dylan Thomas would be.

Voyaging, the minstrels go with chance through the lands of many different peoples. Always they were bound to come across, in the north or the south, some person who is touched by their song and is generous with his gifts... He who works for his own good name will be rewarded on earth by a strong and steady fame.

Dylan Thomas was called a sponger, who lived on the hospitality of others. Yet as a bard, and the greatest bard of Wales since the Middle Ages, that was his right, that was the duty of his hosts to give, if they wished to hear his peerless speech.

He was bestowed the middle name of Marlais by his father. That was the bardic name of his great-uncle William Thomas, called Gwilym Marles, taken from a stream in Cardiganshire. Gwilym was both preacher and bard, a radical and a Unitarian, the champion of Welsh tenants against their landlords, and a leading contributor to the Welsh periodicals of mid-Victorian times. For his support of the poor and the tenants, Gwilym was evicted from his chapel, but he took his flock with him to a new chapel and achieved fame as a defender of the people. He was "the towering dead", remembered in one of Dylan's poems.

Dylan's father, D.J. Thomas, was a potential poet who lived in the no-man's land between the rural bard-and-preacher of the time of Gwilym and the urban rebellious poet, possible in the youth of his son. His struggle to join the middle class and own a villa and bring up a family was too much for his talent at words, which were still-born. As Dylan's wife was to write, D.J. Thomas had to bear the strain of "the transition from farm house and railwaymen standards to schoolmaster in a semi-detached suburban matchbox... from lavish rough comforts to a pinched penny-pricing gentility."

His experience was that of much of Edwardian Wales. The urge of many of the Welsh for respectability at any price would lead to their reputation for hypocrisy. After the preaching of Wesley, much of southern Wales chose puritanism and then a suffocating gentility which was the condition of that blinkered, boxed, never-to-be-forgotten Swansea society, in which Dylan would be born, from which he would flee and rebel, out of which he would never escape.

As he even would complain at the height of his youthful revolt against the stuffy values of his home in Cwmdonkin Drive, all his poetry up to the age of eighteen seemed to have a "terrible lot of priggery in it – intellectual and emotional priggery." It read "like a chunk of adulterated Chesterton revised by Sir Edward Elgar." Childish Dylan could not then renege on the stern strictures of his upbringing.

Oddly enough, Dylan would speak no Welsh and be judged by Nationalists as an Uncle Tom, who wrote the language of the conquerors better than they might. He would inherit the contradictions of the history of his country and his family. His father, who did speak Welsh, refused to teach his son the language, and even felt a certain contempt for those who did speak and write the ancient words. Without question, speaking Welsh at that time in Swansea was a sign of not having quite arrived yet from the valleys or the mountains.

In Cwmdonkin Drive, Dylan's father and mother did not talk in the language of their parents or their youth. As a result, Dylan was steeped in the riches of the English language, although his rhythms and phrasings, his choice of metaphor and odd matchings of words, have that Celtic run and lilt which seems to percolate and press through the greatest writers of Ireland and Wales such as James Joyce and Dylan, both thrushes in an alien tongue that they charm with the magic of their forgotten one.

Dylan's name was his father's choice and it came from the *Mabinogion,* the Old Testament of national myth. In certain ways, that Victorian translation of Celtic legends by Lady Charlotte Guest, the young wife of the self-made master of the Dowlais Ironworks in South Wales, was the inspiration of modern Welsh poetry. In the text, the son of a magician king makes a maiden, who claims to be a virgin, step over a magic wand. She drops a fine male child with yellow hair. Then the son of the magician says: "I shall name this child, and the name I shall give him is Dylan."

Once named, the boy makes for the sea and becomes part of the sea, swimming as fast as the swiftest fish. "And for that reason he was called Dylan Eil Ton, Sea Son of the Wave." Curiously enough, Dylan's wife was to write that he had a definite connection with the fish family with his heavy hulk-shaped head and elongated, utterly useless hands which she was to call fins.

What was interesting in the choice of the son's names by the father was that both Dylan and Marlais were pre-Christian names, both dealt with magic and myth, both were bardic and both had to do with the mystery of the water, the big seas and the rivers of dreams that were to haunt Dylan's imaginings.

This was the heritage of Dylan Thomas. His birthright was a divided country, a divided tradition, a divided language, a divided society, a divided house. As a Welshman, he was born to a land split between the stern nonconformist rural tradition of the naturalist north and the mountains, and the softer English growth of the southern towns and cities. As a bard, he inherited the formal respect for rhyme and discipline of the old court poets, and the opposed gifts of the minstrels, wandering and roistering where they could find ears to hear them.

As a speaker of English, Dylan always had Wales in his blood and heard the waves of Swansea's "two-tongued sea". Such coiled tensions, of course, made the contradictory poet in Dylan, who was indeed "dressed to die" before "the sensual strut began." He was born into conflicts that he could never end except through his work of words, his endless search for a synthesis that was impossible, a unity in divergence, a sweet final resolution of the soul.

Yet how could I adapt Dylan Thomas for anything? If any man ever was meant to be swallowed whole or taken in the round, it was Dylan. With curls on his scalp and red blubber on his lips, thin and young or later bellied and fat, pub-drunk or poet-sober, Dylan was Dylan was Dylan and will be forever amen. Unlike most legends, the legend of Dylan had a lot to do with the fact. And it was quite a rub to get under the skin of a legend and a genius. It was a tight fit to work out what such a wild, yet careful, creator would have done, if he'd completed his unfinished novel and put it on the stage.

Adventures in the Skin Trade was Dylan's only novel. He began it at the outbreak of the Second World War as a fantasy autobiography of his first coming to London. The hero, Sam Bennet, wasn't Dylan; but, as Dylan's friend Vernon Watkins said, "There were to be seven skins. At the end of the story, the character would be naked at last. It would be in one way a journey through the Inferno of London, but it would also be a comedy." This was Dylan's serious intention; but the novel didn't turn out like that. He declared in a self-deprecating way that it blathered on, "a mixture of Oliver Twist, Little Dorrit, Kafka, Beachcomber, and good old 3-adjectives-a-penny belly-churning Thomas, the Rimbaud of Cwmdonkin Drive."

He forgot that the piece was about him being flayed alive, skin by skin. He was carried away by the adjectives of paradise and pub jokes. And the novel petered out after four chapters in a gay bar somewhere in Soho, just as Dylan himself used to puff away his genius on beer froth. Dylan meant to go back to the book and finish it; but the war came and he had to write film scripts for money and he found it hard to pick up the thread. He had let go of the rich and outrageous kite of adolescent fantasy which made the opening of *The Skin Trade* fly so high. The war was too tragic to remember the verve of peace.

I had written a novel about Cambridge called *My Friend Judas*, while I was still an undergraduate there. The prose was influenced by Salinger's *Catcher in the Rye* and Dylan Thomasiana. So when I became a don at the building of Churchill College, I was summoned from my Portakabin to adapt *The Skin Trade* for the stage. All of forty-five years ago, I had a half-finished novel to work with, a First Act that swooped to nowhere and a Second Act dead and buried. My first job was to find Dylan's friends and to get the permission of the Trustees of his estate to work on an adaptation. Soon I was sitting in a bare country house outside Cambridge with John Davenport, Dylan's old companion, as strong as a keg on two legs, and living on a diet of booze and boiled potatoes. He showed me a pile of Dylan's letters and the manuscript of a novel called *The Death of the King's Canary*, in which he and Dylan had written alternate chapters, killing off most of the prewar literary establishment.

On an old typewriter on the kitchen table, we put together the bones of the play according to Dylan's presumed intentions. The seven skins of nature were to be stripped from Sam/Dylan in seven Scenes by the Seven Sins of man, leaving Sam naked at last. The missing three scenes of the Second Act were to take place two years after the First Act; they would show Sam's dissolution and disillusion. Vernon Watkins suggested that Sam should hand round boiled string as Dylan had done at the Surrealist Exhibition of 1936. John Davenport told me about Dylan's going off with a girl, whose head was a rosebush. We made each scene show a sin and the loss of a skin by Sam/Dylan and we left him naked in front of his adopted family, suddenly realizing that the life of pubs and sin was just as suffocating as the life of bourgeois virtue.

At this point, the real Dylan ran away to Wales and married Caitlin Thomas and began the usual cycle of his life. At home, he wrote until "the seven deadly virtues plagued" him to death. Then he ran off for another bout in "the sin – stripping, seven-skin-stripping city." In this cycle between virtue and vice, the country and London, Dylan revolved, slowly "dying of strangers." Then, at last, he crossed the Atlantic, where, as Cyril Connolly once said, he was "mobbed to death, like Orpheus and the Thracian women."

The eventual play of *The Skin Trade* shows Dylan as his fantasy self, Sam Bennet, the innocent exploited by the big metropolis, who is stripped by sins and strangers and goes off bloody, but free to write. It also shows Sam as the young poet on the make, then unmade by sycophants and free drinks and slight notoriety. Yet if the bones of the play are tragic, its flesh is comic. Once we had worked out the skeleton, the best part of my adventure in a dead man's skin over five years of writing and rewriting was the tracking down of jokes and sentences by Dylan to round out the bones.

In *The Death of the King's Canary*, I found a remark of Dylan's that, if he ever became rich, he'd ride a bicycle and have beer for breakfast. Some marvellous phrases came from his stories, some from his radio scripts. Research gave me much of the Surrealists' behaviour in their exhibition, and Vernon Watkins told me that Dylan felt envious there. Fred Janes's account of Dylan's habit of elaborating on a fantastic theme gave me the sequence about being oiled in the oilyverse. A letter to Pamela Hansford Johnson provided Dylan's play plot delivered from the Womb with a View – it was originally called "Spajma and Salnady or Who Shot the Emu?" And Constantine Fitzgibbon's definitive and brilliant biography of Dylan came out just in time for a final touch-up. While I couldn't quote chapter and verse for every remark made by Dylan's characters in the second half of the play, a lot of them were a magpie's hoard of topics about Dylan.

Five years in a dead man's skin makes for a better fit, even if his skin fitted my inadequate body no better than an elephant's hide. Yet if you want to move easily in another's pelt, you have to track down nearly everything he did or wrote. You have to pester his friends and plunder his jottings. The play of *The Skin Trade* was near as I think Dylan would have wanted it to be; it included as much from his pen as I could fit in relevantly. I hoped it showed two important things about him, how the cycle of sin and virtue was the wheel which broke his life, and how friends and strangers killed him.

"Oh God, I'm so tired of sleeping with women I don't even like," Dylan once said to Rayner Heppenstall. When he was asked why he drank too much, he replied, "Because they expect it of me." Like Sam Bennet, Dylan was too easy and passive about his life, though not about his poetry. Things and people happened to him. He could never refuse a free bed or a free drink, until he was flayed alive and ran away to grow his skins again and to write from some inner puritan self the poems that we know.

Vernon Watkins also said, "In Dylan's first plan, so far as I can remember it, there were to be seven skins. At the end of the story the character would be naked at last. It would be in one way a journey through the Inferno of London, but it would also be comedy." In fact, Dylan made a mistake, since he knew his Dante by hearsay. It was a journey through the Purgatory of London, where the young Dylan was successively skinned by the seven deadly sins, leaving him bare and exposed to the seven deadly virtues. The plan was the exposure of the all-embracing naive provincial, Samuel Bennet to the successive corruptions of the Big City. "He would have no money, no possessions, no extra clothes, no civilised bias. And life would come to him … People would come, and they would bring him life. Odd, very odd people would come. But whoever came, and whatever situation came, he would go on. Then at a certain point, an unpredictable point in time, he would look back and find that he had shed a skin."

In fact, the novel was a half-finished reconstruction of Dylan's first visit to London from 1934 to 1936, when he came at the age of twenty and left at twenty-two. In this time, the Welsh Innocent was corrupted in a pattern, which was repeated through the rest of his life. He returned to Laugharne, where he met Caitlin; they went off together, married, and lived an idyll for a time in Cornwall. Dylan would leave this comfort to go whoring and drinking in London, and then return to the increasingly-angry Caitlin for rest and repentance. This pattern would be repeated until his death, In fact, his last seventeen years were a revolving performance of those of his young marriage.

Dylan was fascinated by Marlowe's Faustus, where the Seven Deadly Sins enter. There is Pride, "I disdain to have any parents" : Gluttony, "0, I come of a royal parentage, my grandfather was a gammon of bacon …" : Covetousness, "O, my sweet gold" : Lechery, "Who I, sir? I am the one that loves an inch of raw mutton better than an ell of fried stock-fish …" :

Sloth, "I was begotten on a sunny bank, where I have lain ever since" : Envy, "I cannot read, and therefore wish all books were burnt. I am lean with seeing others eat" : and Wrath, "I had neither father nor mother … ever since I have run up and down the world with this case of rapiers, wounding myself when I had nobody to fight withal. I was born in hell…"

Dylan was also much interested in the mystical elements of the number Seven. "It is what I dream. Seven is a number in magic," says, the madman in 'The Mouse and the Woman'; the girl in 'The Prospect of the Sea' clambers down magically from the seventh short tree; Jarvis says, 'My rose' to his seventh love in 'The Map of Love', but she smelt in his hands'. Seven seems to be, for Dylan, the number which produces his Dream Of Love, which must become corrupted by the Seven Sins, which in turn purge the Artist's soul to make him ready for the poetic vision of heaven, while torturing and killing his body.

But John Davenport died, before we could start writing our collaboration. He was a sad remnant of the redolent bohemian life of the 'thirties and the 'forties, which had been beggared by the Second World War. Once the host of poets and painters, he ended as a drunken giant on a pittance, down on his luck. So I was set on the track of stripping the seven skins of Sam Bennet by the Seven Sins, and making these into scenes for the stage. As it was, the novel filled the First Act, when Sam met and was flayed by the nature of Pride, Gluttony, Covetousness, and Lechery in the Home-Breaking Scene, the Buffet Scene at Paddington Station, the Overstocked Room and Bath Scene, and the Soho Club one. There was a two-year time gap before the Second Act, during which Sam/Dylan had become a minor literary figure.

In the Sloth Sequence of the Fifth Scene, Sam was in the same Soho night club, surrounded by the same 'killing friends' who were to murder him and his talent, the bohemian parasites. He was sick and lazy. His mistress Lucille was there; in real life, he'd caught the clap from her. The following Scene took place at the notorious Surrealist Exhibition of 1936, which first told Dylan how small, provincial and ignorant he was. Lucille was now the mysterious Miss Rosebush, with the flowers all over her face. Sam/Dylan fell for her again, while the famous French Surrealists ignored him.

In the last and Seventh Scene of the original version of my adaption, Sam discovered that Miss Rosebush was an illusion. She was the dressed-up Lucille. He went back to Wales. In fact, he was skinned down to 'bare, forked, unaccommodated man' (Dylan was a great admirer of *King Lear* and tried to live that part in small ways). At this point, he retired to domestic life in Wales with Caitlin Thomas. Later, I rewrote the ending to bring out Dylan's actual engagement to the strait-laced novelist Pamela Hansford Johnson, his final attempt at respectability. As he wrote in 'Lament':

> Now I am a man no more no more,
> And a black reward for a roaring life …
> Modesty hides my thighs in her wings,
> And all the deadly virtues plague my death.

Yet the question remained. Who was to stage *Adventures in the Skin Trade*? And how?

David Hemmings plays the young Dylan in
Adventures in the Skin Trade.

Andrew Sinclair directs John Bird and
Joanna Lumley in *The Breakng of Bumbo*.

David Hemmings draws Samuel Bennet meeting
Mr. Allingham in *Adventures in the Skin Trade*.

David Hemmings in Antonioni's *Blow-Up.*

Joseph von Sternberg, manipulating the
marionette Marlene Dietrich.

ADVENTURES IN THE FILM TRADE

Because of romantic feelings about the incredible city of London, I had always wanted to live in Soho and on the docks and in the Parks, by a Bohemia and the river and the green. Owned by Mrs Fisher, a bargee Queen with cheroot and pin-striped suit and monocle, I discovered in 1964 an abandoned terrace in Narrow Street on the Thames in Limehouse. Blitzed in the Second World War, the dwellings had been built in the eighteenth century by brick and beam, mortar and timber.

I was seduced by the view from the six derelict houses, which still had the barge-builders operating from the cellars. The buildings were set on a wharf on an outer bend of the Thames, so that the eye was carried by the sweep of river towards Greenwich on the left and Tower Bridge on the right. Facing me across the Thames, two factory chimneys made a rifle's foresight to aim the view, while day-and-night sounds of machinery and wreaths of smoke flew with the gulls and the swans over the water from the working of ENTHOVEN and ESSO on Lavender Wharf. Around them, gutted ruins, and a rubbish tip, where trucks emptied wastes down canvas chutes into barges to be towed away.

On either side of the river, warehouses squatted and bulked below the arms and torsos of the cranes, which were spiders in the blue fog of the morning or else were dragonflies in the low slant of the evening sun. Below, on the north foreshore, the long coffins of the Thames barges had slats over their maws and red-painted decks, still the same size as the galleons, which had been made there in the first Queen Elizabeth's time, when Walter Raleigh had sailed off to found Roanoke, and when the whole of North American history had been a dream of adventurers seeking Eldorado from this East End of London town.

Scrubby tugs also lay on the gravel bank, their hatches lime-green, navy-blue-funnelled, rust-arsed and ready for reconditioning to leave a cleaner wake. At the end of the buildings, the back of a pub called *The*

Grapes (Charles Dickens drank here) and beyond, another great chimney of a power station, smutting the air so that black rain fell on the twin giant cranes that walked away downriver into the last light, two red lamps shining at the edge of their platform. To the west, the river crooked its vein into the heart of the City, with a Wren church spire pushing up its white bill in the midst of a nest of the iron-boned cranes. On the rim, Tower Bridge held up its two manacled wrists, while the street-lamps dressed themselves in single file to confine the water o'nights.

Such mystery and brutality of place, such stark demand of beauty, such harsh vision, made me decide to keep a hidden place there for my writing. And when the long narrow studio was finished, with its white-painted pine walls leading out to a balcony that jutted over the tidal Limehouse Reach, I could stand on my rope-caulked deck and steer like Captain Ahab towards the two chimneys across the river, when the storms hammered at the skylights and the barges banged against the wooden watergate of the house, trembling like *The Victory* at anchor before Trafalgar.

Then I knew why I was there, playing the sea-dog at the muddy ditch from where England had grown to Empire, black factories, coal-dark bricks, iron ships, the docks of London, where any sailor could drop down in the foc's'le in a cone of yellow light from the deck lamps and begin as Conrad's Marlow to say: "A funny thing happened to me on my way to Penang last voyage…"

I would watch the great cargo ships from the four corners of the world, as they were towed beside the wharves by the tugs. Sometimes I saw a couple of floating cranes move slowly past, hanging the low sun on the gibbets of their frame, the *London Hercules* and the *London Titan*, as Lady Life-in-Death's skeletal ship in *The Ancient Mariner*. Once I saw a red-sailed Thames lugger, drifting a bloody patch towards Greenwich; once a four-masted clipper training ship; once even a painted galleon, again as the craft of Samuel Taylor Coleridge, mysteriously making towards the sea without noise or sails, by opening the air in front and closing it behind, presumably set on course for the new gold mines of film sets in Spain.

Most evenings, in the decay of trade and night and main, there were just some bumping tugs, pulling strings of barges loaded with bales of old paper, or a few lighters croaking their way across to France, or some navy cadets toiling at the oars in whalers on water too dirty even for a shrimp to survive in, or perhaps cold youths in racing-sculls, which made a plaything of this foul river that had once floated counter-Armadas. For the little diesel freighters of rebuilt Rotterdam were now taking most of the cargoes of the continent away from the London docks, as Europe slowly began to unite and Britain stayed on her cold island, waiting for destiny to visit again, giving her another opportunity, or else carrying her away.

Limehouse was, indeed, the finale of the imperial theatre, its docks deserted, half its houses fallen into a wasteland of bomb-sites, a whole generation of dockers neglected by even Labour governments, which knew what a safe seat it was in the House of Commons. If violence was the theme of the time, this slum certainly was rich in aggressions, with memories of the Chinese gang wars and Jack the Ripper's murders and now the bullyboys of Cable Street and the Kray brothers, still terrorizing the turf of rubble. The local version of shooting grouse on moors was potting rats with air-rifles on the gravel foreshore or cornering them with terriers in the barges, where the excitement of the bloodbath led to one famous docker biting off the heads of the rodents – until his false teeth slipped.

There was none of the proletarian nostalgia of Arnold Wesker's plays in the East End. The dockers all marched for Enoch Powell, when he warned against the rising tide of immigration to Britain. "What, Andrew," they said to me in the pub "you never shared a toilet with them?" I had not often, but when I pointed out there must be only three or four immigrants among the ten thousand registered London dockers, many of whom had worked on unloading ships for generations, they thought I had missed the point. They wanted to have no competition, to keep things as they were. And I knew that the word 'comrade' did not always extend beyond the white cliffs of Dover.

A journalist, called Carole d'Albiac, came to interview me at the time. Her description was pretty accurate.

> He lives in a flat in Soho Square and a house in Limehouse, which he is converting, surrounded by the Belle Epoque; toy Japanese soldiers, busts of famous feminists, Lautrec posters, musical boxes and instruments, a black mobile paper bird, old watches that he is making into a musical box, horses from fairgrounds, more posters. He wears old clothes in sombre

colours, doesn't always bother to shave, drives an old mini-van, drinks whisky. His conversation is scattered with quotations – within a few hours from Plato, Simone de Beauvoir, Sartre, Freud, Kennedy, Mary Wollstonecraft, Conrad, Proust, Marx. He needs to eat and sleep less frequently than most people. He likes to be alone and discover his natural rhythm. When he is tired of sitting in one room writing, watching ships go by and the light on the water, he knocks down a wall, moves earth or plans a room. He listens intently to what people are saying, looks very mournful if the conversation is not intelligent, and very cross if, at the end of an argument, his opponent says he doesn't believe in argument, anyway.

At that time, a Cambridge friend, the playwright Michael Frayn, said of me: "He's craggy. His long, rather sad face, lights up and becomes animated. He's very telegenic. I always thought that, like Jonathan Miller, he had the power, when you were discussing something, to make it romantic." I doubt any small screen presence, but I am incurably romantic. And I have always tried to make a practical matter of my reveries.

My wife of the time, Marianne, also said that of me. "He isn't satisfied to leave hopes, projects and ambitions at the dream stage. Sooner or later, when someone tells him that their secret dream is to make films, climb Mount Everest, go back to law school or become a Bedouin, Andrew very sincerely asks, 'Why don't you?' and proceeds to demonstrate that it's perfectly feasible, and offers help. And he really does convince people sometimes to try again, that it's not too late."

Alas, I have tried too often to prove that only the impossible ever happens. And yet, without that belief, how may we ever achieve more than we are capable of doing? Certainly, there was next to no chance of putting onstage *Adventures in the Skin Trade*. Then the innovative director James Roose-Evans picked up my draft of Dylan's squib in my agent's office. He optioned it for a production at the small Hampstead Theatre. He set me to work on the script, and he was kind about my ability to rewrite:

"Andrew's marvellously objective and professional. Even if he has spent days working on an idea, if I ever say I don't like it, he just grins and tears it up. You can have a really creative relationship with him. He has steeped himself in everything Dylan ever wrote or said. He's really got inside the skins."

In the case of *Adventures in the Skin Trade*, by choice and improbability, one actor stopped treading the boards to star in the movies, while another was consigned to parts that never revealed his full potential. The first was David Hemmings, the second was Terence Stamp, who turned down my leading role. Hemmings was broke and came to lodge with me in Limehouse. He was dynamic and hilarious and irrepressible, as beautiful as a fallen angel, as rackety as Punch-and-Judy on the pier. Because we couldn't stage the first scene, when Sam Bennet smashes up his Swansea home and leaves for London, I shot it as a Keystone comedy in black-and-white on my 16mm Bolex, with Hemmings cavorting and his agent John Daley – later of Hemdale production fame – carrying the camera legs for two pounds from his client's twenty pounds a week. And while filming an East End whore against the brick wall of my riverside cellar, Clare Peploe walked in with a mysterious Italian gentleman. "Too busy," I said, "go upstairs. I am filming."

I should try to explain about Clare Peploe, although no explanation would ever be able to elucidate that enigma variation. Her grandfather was a renowned Scots painter, her father ran an art gallery, while her quick quirk of a smile and withdrawn passion made her so elusive that she was pursued by many a hunter. I lost her once on too long a walk over the Borders in order to write my only major novel *Gog*, before returning to find her gone. We had grappled briefly on a *chaise-longue* among the running rats in an unbuilt corner of Narrow Street.

Sweet Thames, run hotly, till I end my song.

Now, exquisitely beautiful with green-wide eyes that glanced away in evasion, another Monica Vitti of mystery, she had brought Michelangelo Antonioni to see me. For him, she was scouting the sets for *Blow-Up*. When I found out who was with her, I blushed. I had told him to wait – *I* was filming. He was charming and murmured something about Dylan and "*certezza d'amore*". Looking at him and Clare, I didn't think I had much hope of that.

"Translate, Clare," he said. "Translate." She danced on the bare caulked boards, and then she clawed at his sleeve, and said: "It is better not to love at all, than to love without certainty."

I have never gone for introspection and self-analysis, nor even do I describe the motives of the characters in my novels. I have always been a sort of existentialist. By our behaviour and our deeds are we known. I was most fortunate that David Hemmings described me before he died, in those days of our adventures together:

> Although the play was based on works by Dylan Thomas, it was adapted for the stage by Andrew Sinclair, a man of great singularity who was to have a profound influence on my future. He was also one of the most eccentric people I've ever met.
>
> Andrew was an Old Etonian, a dour academic who gave the impression of being in a permanent state of mental trauma, as if the world might collapse under the weight of his thoughts. He was a highly regarded historian who'd published much fine work, but he dressed like an extra in a Spaghetti Western with that sort of studied rumpledness which only a top wardrobe designer could have concocted. His suits, when he wore them, looked like rejects from the Fifty Shilling Tailor, and his shirts had wide, unbuttoned collars, loosely held together by drab ties in vast Windsor knots.
>
> His extraordinary, triangular brow, furrowed like an ill-ploughed field, seemed to stretch several feet up to a great pink dome, topped by a few dark strands of hair, cascading wildly. Below, a glorious hooter swept in a great Gothic curve from brow to lower lip. From the depths beneath when he spoke, there emerged a grumbling murmur, like a volcano with a sore throat, while a floppy lower lip burbled in harmony, as if plucked from the point of his chin.
>
> It was an amazing visage, but believe me, I couldn't have written the last couple of paragraphs if I hadn't adored him. He was an utterly unique man in whose Hindenburg head lay seams of knowledge I could only dream of. His adaptation of Dylan

Thomas is a stunning work. Not only because it translates Thomas so well to the stage, but also because it does this with elegance, and a patina of nonsense the poet himself would have recognised and admired.

I invited Clare to the First Night at the Hampstead Theatre. As usual, she hardly spoke, certainly not of what was happening in her life, and then she rapidly disappeared. David Hemmings was incandescent in what I believe was the greatest performance of his career – glittering as the comet he would become with a comic timing almost worthy of Chaplin. The reviews were good, and we looked forward to a transfer after three weeks to the West End. In *The Guardian*, "The poet comes to London, bewildered, over-articulate, shock-headed with a beer-bottle hopelessly stuck on his finger. His encounters are farcical, raucous and touching." In *The Financial Times*, "A superb piece of effervescent writing, pullulating with anecdote, caricature and life lived at a pace that would lay most men flat after an hour or two." And in *The Telegraph*, "Based on Lewis Carroll – Dylan in Blunderland – deliciously funny, a faithful blend of ribald sadness and unconventional good cheer."

Without telling me, Clare took Antonioni to the Second Night. He was thunderstruck by the lightning and the gall of the Hemmings performance. That night, David was summoned to Claridge's, where Clare stood behind a red curtain to hear the audition for *Blow-Up*. Terence Stamp was fired, Hemmings was hired. The moral was, if there was one: – always take a good part, even at four fivers a week. You never know who will come and see you at the theatre. As it was, the producer Carlo Ponti bought the penniless David a white Rolls Royce *coupé*, and he drove away from Limehouse with more pomp than the neighbouring gangster Kray brothers.

As we had lost our star, we never did reach the West End. Yet David was also to give his iconic film performance as the hip photographer in *Blow-Up*; while Vanessa Redgrave played Clare's indecipherable self, saying to Hemmings with his camera: "My private life's already in a mess. It would be a disaster if …", only to hear his reply, "So what – nothing like a little disaster for sorting things out."

Years later, when I reached Hollywood, and Antonioni was filming *Zabriskie Point* in Death Valley, I read in the *Los Angeles Times* that, between takes, the Italian Director would climb a salt hill to talk to an alone and anonymous blonde, watching the climax, the explosion that shattered a ranch-house. I thought I knew who she might be. And on seeing Clare again for lunch on a rare return to London, I asked her about Death Valley. For once, in her coming and going, she would talk about Michelangelo. "Yes, it was I. He had twenty cameras ready to record that big blow-up. He said, Was I satisfied? No, I said. I wanted him to blow up all America."

He could not hold Clare. She would quit him for another director, Bernardo Bertolucci. Freud once wrote that, after analysing women for thirty years, he still did not know what they wanted. Clare would always search for some perfection that she could never attain. But in leaving me and going off with Antonioni and taking David Hemmings with them after the run of *Adventures In The Skin Trade*, she was not aware that others had seen the play, and I would be translated elsewhere.

Although Antonioni had taken David Hemmings away from me, Tennessee Williams had also seen the play and had pronounced it the best one in London, although he probably only fell for David's beauty and charisma, as we all did. Lester Persky had been backing Tennessee theatrically at that time and had decided to expand into making films. He bought an option on my property for very little and also my services as a screenwriter for not much more. And after a hard day's night in a bar, he got David to sign a paper napkin saying that he would play the lead in the film for a few silver peanuts. All without reference to our agents, of course.

When I had finished my screenplay, I took it at noon to Lester, who was staying at Claridge's. I found him lying on the floor on his back, his legs upstretched on a soft chair. "It's my spine," he said. "But I have ordered breakfast." At a knock, I opened the door of the suite, so that a waiter could totter forward with a silver platter, holding a cornucopia of goodies, and lay the vast metal dish on the marble table by the bedside. A wail of anguish rose from Lester's lips, and he sat bolt upright. "Goddamit," he said. "You've put it on my contact lenses." So when I presented my script to him, he said he obviously couldn't read it. And when I asked him for my advance money on delivery, he told me to wait.

"Now you've signed and delivered," he said to me, "let's renegotiate."

This was a new proposition to me. I had thought a contract was a contract.

"But we have agreed, Lester," I said.

"You have agreed," Lester said. "But I have not yet signed. And once I have agreed and signed, I still have to pay you. So let's renegotiate."

Such was a valuable lesson in how to secure a property, a screenplay and a star for a few thousand dollars. Watch the fringe theatre, pick up the rising writer and the future star, sign them cheaply out of reach of their advisers. Insist on personal negotiations. If not, no deal. Something signed on a serviette is perfectly binding in a court of law. You can wipe an agent's nose on it. Actually, Lester lost on the deal, because he never made the film of *Adventures in the Skin Trade*. Doubtless, he wrote off his expenses, for he went on to become an expert at tax-loss investments in films and produced many good movies through his company, Persky Bright.

He had though, like Lord Nelson, a blind eye in picking out the signals of the stars to be. When we were trying to put the stage version of Dylan's novel on at *The Circle in the Square* in Greenwich Village, Lester took me to see another little-known young American actor, then playing the lead in Henry Livings's *Eh!* It was a fine performance, but Lester and Ted Mann, the theatrical manager, shook their heads. "He's not big enough," they agreed. "Not big enough to carry a Broadway show." The actor's name was Dustin Hoffman. It was just before he was chosen to play in the film of *The Graduate*. If Lester had signed him up on a Babe Ruth candybar wrapping paper to play the lead in our film, we could have set our terms for making it, after a year or two.

The hopeful film producer with a little to spend in mounting a movie must have a nose like a truffle pig and a touch like a fly fisherman. The scent of the right property, the feel for the coming writer and the future star is a deal in store. With instinct and flair – and twenty thousand dollars or less – a producer can put together a package wrapped in gold gift-paper, worth a ten million dollar budget or more.

When I was to reach Hollywood, I found that I was already notorious. I was the man who did not know Frank Sinatra. Writing *Gog* alone in the docks for a couple of summers between teaching at University College, London, I was rather off my head, wandering in my mind in the mists and myths of ancient Albion. In a rare stint as a film producer, Sinatra had come to Britain to make a picture, *The Naked Runner*. One scene was set on the Rhine; but opposite my river house on the Thames was a factory sign, *ENTHOVEN*. By cheating a shot from my balcony, a small fortune could be saved from the budget. Frank himself was playing a good guy, who was turned into an assassin, but he needed my old grey river with Ma Fisher's moored barges, to keep his film rolling along.

In mid-flow and paragraph, I heard a front man hammering on my street door. Would I accept a hundred pounds from Sinatra to shoot from my house? I swore, and said I was writing. Never taking no for an answer and presuming that my poverty was greater than my pride, the Sinatra gang returned a week later with several movie vans and black limousines, and they set up shop in the nearby pub, *The Black Horse.* Again the front man hammered at my door. "Would *two* hundred pounds ...?" "Get out, I'm writing!"

The landlord of the pub later told me a furious discussion broke out in *The Black Horse* about what to do. Teach me a lesson? Or go to the Rhine? That would be at least another hundred thousand pounds on the budget. There was only one solution. Protesting and livid with anger, Frank Sinatra himself walked across Narrow Street and banged on my dusty door. Furious at a second intervention that morning, I ran down the stairs to open up. Hardly noticing the small shape in front of me and barely hearing his words, "I'm Frank Sinatra, and I would like to...", I screamed at him, "I'm writing. I never heard of you."

I was told that an incandescent Sinatra went back to the pub and told the goons that always went with him to take me out. For once, they advised caution. Wasn't this the territory of Jack the Ripper? Hadn't George Raft been deported, because of his gangster connections? And I must be a personal friend of the ferocious East Enders, the Kray brothers, or I would never dare defy Sinatra like that. A week later, I heard a commotion a few ruined balconies downriver, and there they all were, filming *The Naked Runner.* My yells for peace and quiet were quelled by the estuary breeze. Only later did I know my madness had bought me a smidgeon of fame.

I had met a charismatic young film director, Peter Lorrimer Whitehead. I was earning big money, he was not. He sucked me into his venture of publishing screenplays, which he began by turning out in print and picture the *Alphaville* of Jean-Luc Godard. He also involved me in backing his film productions, one with the Rolling Stones, *Tonite, Let's Make Love in London.* Always in love with himself, Peter had to produce, direct, write and star in his own movies. As a minimal Orson Welles, Peter was certain that he was a one-man masterpiece.

I have a practical insanity within me. I like to turn my obsessions into going concerns. Peter wanted to sell out to me, I wanted to print classic screenplays. I knew nothing about how publishing worked, and I still know very little. Anyway, I was making too much money, rewriting film scripts in Hollywood. I used to hate myself out there in Beverley Hills and Bel Air – those plush rooms, that mortal loneliness, the death-dealing in the Polo Lounge. All the while, I creaked out the words, which were slowly read and hardly approved. Over the weeks, I felt futile, corrupt and isolated.

These appalling interludes culminated in a restaurant called the Brown Derby. It was 1968, the blacks were burning down the ghetto of Watts, I was on the only hotline between Hollywood and Cuba, where my wife Marianne had gone to present a baby to Castro's Revolution, and I had had quite enough. Rather as in Graham Greene's *Our Man in Havana*, the monitored telephone presumed 'baby' meant 'bomb', and I was already being followed by a CIA football squad. The snickering Vice-President of some studio or another informed me that George Raft owned the restaurant. If I didn't get my words right, I would be knee-capped.

"How much do I owe you?" I said.

Surprised, he said, "Twenty-five thousand dollars."

I wrote him out a cheque and handed it to him.

"Twenty-five thousand dollars," I said. "And now I will tell you what I think of you."

He looked at the cheque in wonder. "Writers don't return money," he said.

"This one does," I said. And then I told him that I hoped the blacks would not only burn down Watts, but the whole of bloody Los Angeles. This had something to do with free speech. The VP smiled, and he folded up my cheque and put it in his pocket.

"You'll never work here again," he said.

"I don't want to," I said. And left. And never did.

I was, indeed, blacklisted soon for my Cuban connections. Whatever rash choices I have made have spurted from my two main sins, wrath and pride. I watch with astonishment the results of my actions. As Dylan Thomas said, "Temperamental? It's ninety per cent temper and ten per cent mental."

In the course of all this, I wrote a quickfire sonnet about being a screenwriter:

Sow's ears I could not make into silk purses,
No pearls I cast before the stars and swine.
I'd smile and say to Hollywood producers,
"I'll give you *sold* sow's ears, but dead on time.

"You want it good and Tuesday? At the best,
"You'll get what Liz can say and Roy can shoot."
I was the fastest pen in all the West,
My six-gun blasted words to stack their loot.

They had a double talk I learned too late,
"Now that you've signed the contract, got us set,
And done the script, we'll renegotiate."
"But why?" "Because we haven't paid you yet."

The man who tries to pander to his art
Discovers prostitutes are twice as smart.

I used to say I wrote bad screenplays, in order to print good ones. Over twenty years, we quite invented the genre and published some seventy-five classic scenarios by directors such as Orson Welles and Kurosawa, Eisenstein and Lang, Bergman and Bunuel, Carné and Vigo, Hitchcock and Ford, Antonioni and Pasolini, Erich von Stroheim and Pabst, W.C. Fields and the Marx Brothers and Satyajit Ray. I met many of the makers; Jean Renoir, tubby in a check suit; Truffaut, as subtle as a dissolve between night and day; and Roman Polanski, whom Kenneth Tynan rightly described as "the five-foot Pole you wouldn't touch a barge with." The two, who stick in my memory, were Josef von Sternberg and Jean-Luc Godard..On my scripting *safaris* to Hollywood, I worked with Sternberg on *The Blue Angel*. Bald and short and authoritarian, he told me exactly what to do and what he had done. His favourite exhibit was a cartoon of himself, manipulating a wooden doll of Marlene Dietrich on wires. As he wrote in the introduction to the screenplay;

> Film actors, as all students of film history know, are nothing more than glorified marionettes. But unlike a real puppet-master, the director of a film does not manipulate strings on expressionless puppets. For him the dolls are extraordinary

personalities who are prone to move every muscle of face and figure to demonstrate every awkward emotion. And when the strings are manoeuvred to present acceptable masks, there is dismay and rebellion. What to reveal and what to conceal is the function of the director.

As for discovering Marlene Dietrich, for once he said it was not himself.

"I am not an archaeologist who finds some buried bones with a pelvis that indicates a female. I am a teacher who took a beautiful woman, instructed her, presented her carefully, edited her charms, disguised her imperfections and led her to crystallize a pictorial aphrodisiac. She was a perfect medium, who with intelligence absorbed my direction, and despite her own misgivings responded to my conception of a female archetype. The balance of the players did as they were told."

In a letter, Sternberg said he liked me very much and advised not too much furious work. "Don't. It is unwise. Your perspective vanishes. Your energy with it." By the end of my many years with Lorrimer Publishing, we would do seven Godard films, the last two being *Weekend* and *Wind from the East*. Over these, I met him. He was back to filming with an Arriflex on his shoulder in London, and he had run out of money. He was making a movie about continual revolutions; it starred Mao and Guevara and the Rolling Stones, recording *Sympathy for the Devil*. In a surreal ending, he acted as a deranged director, sending off a black man and a blood-painted white woman with guns on a cinematic dolly into the air.

As I was sitting in my Soho office, a small man in an old brown mackintosh emerged through the door. Announcing himself as Godard, he asked me how much money we had in the bank. I looked at a statement. For once it was more black than red.

"Eleven hundred pounds," I said.

"Next Wednesday," he said. "I want it all. Used five pound notes. In a brown paper bag. What films do you want of mine?"

I took the two previous revolutionary ones, and I went to my branch. When I asked for all the money we had in used fivers, I was regarded with deep suspicion. Drug-dealing? Money laundering? Only Godard was taking me to the cleaners. I knew the story of him, cracking the safe of his

French producer, who would not come up with the necessary. I drew up our simple two-page contract, for that was all it was in those days of trust, and I waited for his appearance.

Looking extremely seedy, Godard sidled through the door. I handed him the paper bag of cash.

"Would you like to count it, *m'sieu* Godard?" I asked.

He shook his head. Revolutionary honour was at stake.

"What do I have to sign?"

I gave him the short terms of agreement.

"Would you like to read it?"

Again he shook his head. He signed the second page, and he turned to go.

"Pardon, m'sieu Godard," I said. "But I feel as if I am in one of your films. A bank heist, I believe."

At last, I achieved a smile from the great man on his way out.

"Peut-être" was his last line, although I was reminded of Willie Sutton's reply, when asked why he had robbed so many banks, "Because that's where the money is".

My other highlight was working with Graham Greene on the publication of the script of *The Third Man*, with all its cuts and emendations. The film called on the genius of an extraordinary quartet, Graham Greene and Carol Reed and Orson Welles and Alexander Korda. It set a particular style for British films, a combination of realism of background and penetration of character, based on the two main qualities of the British wartime cinema, a feeling for documentary detail and social purpose. Carol Reed explained the success of the film, shot in 1949, by saying that it was one of the first British films allowed to be made chiefly on location. Until that time, making films in studios had falsified and glamourised all.

In this film, the wet, brooding labyrinths of ruined and occupied Vienna express the traps and ambiguities facing people there, the harsh and shifting choices forced on the survivors of the war. Men plot out their little schemes in front of an arras of urban disaster. Harry Lime scuttling across the bomb-sites, the small operator trying to get rich on the surface of a total waste, is the symbol of the futility of shrewdness in the face of devastation. Lime tries to exploit war and shortages; he dilutes the life-giving penicillin until it gives death. But he is caught in the same vicious circle and in a closed city; as the British Military Policeman Calloway says, "A rat would have more chance in a closed room without a hole and a pack of terriers loose." War and its aftermath crushes all individuals, however clever they may be. And Orson Welles invented his most famous view on history on the Big Wheel:

> "In Italy for thirty years under the Borgias they had warfare, terror, murder, bloodshed – they produced Michelangelo, Leonardo da Vinci and the Renaissance. In Switzerland they had brotherly love, five hundred years of democracy and peace, and what did that produce...? The cuckoo clock. So long, Holly."

In the course of printing *The Third Man*, I was told a splendid story about one of Korda's screenwriters, entering the office of the maestro and demanding to be paid. "We had a gentleman's agreement," the offended author said. "Looking round this room," Korda replied, "I see only one gentleman in it." This tale was capped by the actress Beatrice Lillie, knocking on the boudoir door of Noel Coward at his Blue Harbour house in Jamaica. "Do you have a gentleman in your bed?" she inquired politely. "Just a minute," he replied. "I'll ask him." But then, he was not speaking only for himself.

At any rate, after two years of wordsmithing at the Hollywood anvil, I had the money to pursue my wildest dream. In 1970, I bought a two-year option for £2,000 against £20,000 on the first day of shooting a film of the masterpiece by Dylan Thomas, his Play for Voices, *Under Milk Wood*. The odds against actually producing anything from this poetic torment of phrases was blowing in the storm. And indeed, the widowed Caitlin had emigrated to Italy to marry a Southerner from a clannish family.

So when the agent for the Dylan Estate, the wily David Higham, announced to her the news of this huge sum to be paid for the film rights of the radio play, he was forced to fly out to Rome and beyond to get her to sign the contract. Her new husband was vastly suspicious. His wife would sign only on his mother's bones. Higham swore that I was genuine and that the money would be paid.

A marble urn was produced, the oath was accepted, the deal was approved by Caitlin. And as against all the odds, the film of *Under Milk Wood* would be made and the full £20,000 paid – a fortune in those days

– I found myself the sugar-daddy of Caitlin's children, quite footing the bills for their education. It was apt. As Dylan had been my tutor, so I should see his offspring through school.

Dylan and Caitlin Thomas

Dylan directing *Under Milk Wood* in New York.

TO BEGIN AT AN UNLIKELY BEGINNING

In making *Under Milk Wood*, luck exceeded incredulity and vanished into Celtic mist. Like a necromancer juggling the elements, any Merlin of the screen has to mix the gold of the backers with the stars in their courses and come up with a horoscope that guarantees fair heavens and a safe return. To go at all, *Under Milk Wood* had to find a time when Richard Burton, Elizabeth Taylor, and Peter O'Toole were all available to work and in England, which was rather like fixing a week-end between Howard Hughes, Queen Elizabeth the Second and Puck. Then the gold had to be conjured in double-quick time from the state and a merchant bank, both of whom were rightly foolish enough to buck the wisdom of Wardour Street and think there could be profit as well as art in the wild warm words of that people's poet, Dylan Thomas.

Later, I was asked how I had collected together 'the Debrett of Welsh acting' to perform for £200 a week or less in *Under Milk Wood* – David Jason and Ruth Madoc, Vivian Merchant and Sian Phillips, and a host of others. I replied that they had collected me. I was sitting in my Soho office, when Glynis Johns knocked at my door. She had heard on the grapevine, or should I say pintaphone, that Dylan's masterpiece was to be made.

"Would you give me a part?" she asked in that trembling husky voice of hers. "Any part."

"Any part you want," I said. "I've been in love with you since I was seventeen."

So she played Myfanwy Price, the sweetshop keeper, in love with the draper Mog Edwards, represented by Victor Spinetti in their heart-shaped dreams. The ever-young Angharad Rees, as the not-so-prim schoolteacher Gossamer Beynon, was the only one to play in both my Thomas films, later as his wife Caitlin in a biopicture *Dylan On Dylan*.

All the actors were under the spell of that enchanter of words, whose voice seemed to sing through all their voices in an incantation to the incessant soundings in every village there ever was.

There is a necessity in a film, once it has begun, which matches the resignation in a Celt, once he has decided to go for broke. There are so many shots to be taken each day, so many actors to play their scenes while they are still available, so many seconds of film to be put successfully in the can each week – or else, the boot. Considerations of art come a bad second to sheer endurance. One makes the script and hopes it works. Any improvisation on the set is a dangerous gift that may save the part, but throw the whole. The important thing, as Beckett once wrote, is to be done, to have done. And to have done well. For there are no excuses. A film-maker is judged by the final film. He can plead none of his troubles on the way, too little time, bad weather, fractious actors, intervention from the money, accident. The final cut is all.

Yet endurance and luck are not enough to make a good film. There has to be magic as well. And magic is not on call. For me, *Under Milk Wood* has always been the supreme incantation of my life. However many hundred times I heard the words during the tedious repetitions of editing and dubbing a film, the phrases still reverberated in a tease of meanings as only the great sentences do. Richard Burton would complain of being woken o'nights by voices haunting him with Dylan's words; but his own voice with its fits and starts, graduations and gravels, choirs and harmonies was the midnight speech of the lost Bards of Wales. The magic began when he recorded the sullen craft of his dead friend's words in two hours in a Soho cellar before the picture started. We always had that spell to play back to ourselves during the bad days, and every time we heard it, the magic came again and we thought that *Under Milk Wood* might work after all.

Daring to make a classic like Dylan's is a fool's leap into the dark wood. The arrogance of setting forth our own visual imagination on a screen to compete with the dreams of the many followers of the poet with their own dark-bright visions from the words alone invited divine destruction. Yet our insolence somehow seemed to amuse the Welsh gods. If they did not forgive us, they played with us obscurely, and through their fatal nudging, they brought the magic into the film. If I can try to describe what was beyond sense …

The problem of making Dylan's radio play into a film lay in its bittiness, cross-cutting from voice to voice all the time without knowing whose voice it was. Seventy little stories to tell in ninety minutes in the life of a small fishing-port. The connecting link was Two Voices, their characters and connection with the town unexplained, Voices with the power to conjure up dreams, knowing intimately the private lives of all the sleepers in Cockle Row and Coronation Street, godlike in their comprehension and devilish in their mockery. How to make this counterpoint of words into one visual whole, while being faithful to the text. . . It was daunting.

I had only half-solved the problem when we began shooting the film. I had given the Two Voices faces and characters, predominance to the powerful, brooding face and pale-piercing eyes of Richard Burton, foolery to the thin, playful, melancholic skull's head of Ryan Davies, the beloved clown of Welsh television, playing the jester to Burton's King, the imp to Lucifer. I had gone back to an early experience of Dylan's, when he had spent a weekend with a friend in Gower, and the friend's girl with a loose red mouth had swapped beds. I had also gone back to Dylan's other great radio piece, *Return Journey*, in which the old Dylan travels home to look for the young Dylan, and the final refrain is the same as in Polly Garter's song..." dead, dead, dead." There was also a story of his called *Just Like Little Dogs*, where two men take out two sisters on the beach and the girls change partners in the night. So I made the reason for the Two Voices going back to Llaregyb their quest for a girl, Norma Jane Jenkins, whom they had met way back in the war, and had shared; it made for nice intercutting with the children's kissing games, Billy and Johnnie Cristo and Dicky kissing Gwennie, and with Polly Garter's song as she scrubs the floor of the Welfare Hall:

> *"Tom, Dick, and Harry were three fine men*
> *And I'll never have such loving again..."*

Then Norma Jane walks away into a graveyard and the men leave town in their khaki coats, and it is revealed that Norma Jane has been dead a long time, and that these two visible spirits from the sea and the dark wood have come back to relive their life in the timeless town and resurrect their lost love.

At that time, I was close to the lovely and elegant literary agent Pat Kavanagh. With her red hair and green eyes and darting mind, she wished to become an actress. And how could I deny her? The actors' union Equity could. So I gave her part no lines and only a walk-on or lay-down presence. As the script declared that Norma Jane would be naked between the amorous Two Voices, for an interview with me, Equity sent round four actresses, ready to bare their breasts. I said to each of them:

"No, madam, *Under Milk Wood* is not quite the Windmill Theatre. Please remain covered."

Yet I was prejudiced and I did not cast them. I had the privilege of putting Kavanagh on the screen as an Extra without pay. I flouted no union rules. She would be wonderful in her part, wearing one of her mannish suits, this time in khaki to suggest the time of the Second World War. There was nothing of the casting couch in it, only a willing admiration. And as she was made to say in her later obituary, she did get to snog Richard Burton, while wearing a skin-tight slip.

Another friend I cast was Vivien Merchant as the horrid Mrs Pugh. She was then married to Harold Pinter. I was a neighbour of theirs in Hanover Terrace in Regent's Park. Because she usually had the glacial reserve of somebody in a Pinter play with more pause than patter, I once said to her:

"Speaking or not speaking as you do, Vivien, I almost believe you write Harold's plays."

"People think I do," she said, while Harold only gave a tight grin.

I used to see Harold alone from time to time about making films. Once I went to visit him with Max Rosenberg, a dandy, slate-eyed film producer, who had given me his view of New York. "The third law of thermodynamics operates there. *Chuzpah* does better than talent." At our interview, Harold was quivering. "Ah," Max said later, "he can be like that. A flung knife."

Max had produced *The Birthday Party*, before taking to making Horror Movies, for the money. At a rough cut of the Pinter film, he had complained of a long silence in a scene. Harold then said: "It stays. *(pause)*. I know. *(long pause)*. I wrote it." Once he came to dinner along with Gregory Peck and William Golding, before he won *his* Nobel Prize. "I would have accepted sooner," Harold told me with his usual grace, "if I had known Bill Golding was coming." His rudeness was in defence of his privacy – no chips on his shoulders, only a resentment of any intrusion.

After putting Vivien Merchant into *Under Milk Wood*, occasionally I went down the Nash Terrace to drink champagne with them in the evenings. When Harold departed with Antonia Fraser, a dishevelled Vivien might arrive for a glass or five, before I escorted her back home before her early death. By a quirk of fate, I took my abiding wife, Sonia Melchett, off Antonia's previous husband, Hugh Fraser. Their children had all expected Sonia to become their stepmother, but instead, they had Harold as their stepfather, and unexpectedly, a very good stepfather he turned out to be. He seemed to have been missing a large family all his life. He could not rage, rage against the living of the young. And when our criss-crossed quartet finally met after dinner at the Caprice, we never discussed what had happened. "The past of the four of us," Sonia wisely said, "is too much in the present to talk about it."

As for David Jason, he was born with a leer in his mouth and a wink in his eye. For the first time, my brilliant casting director, Miriam Brickman, told me to go down to Cardiff for two days of auditions. Most of the flock of Welsh actors had never been in a film before, but I could see their talents shine through for every small role in the film. And such was the multitude of talents that selection was extremely difficult. For the part of Nogood Boyo, however, Jason was matchless, the ultimate wheeler-dealer and sexy pop-eyed rogue, very like a caricature of Dylan himself, and the Del Boy of the future.

As for Peter O'Toole, among the stars I found him the meteor. Witty and irrepressible, unpredictable and daring, he taught me that life is mostly coincidence, and action is all. I first met him, when he was cast by Tony Richardson to play the lead at the Royal Court in the musical version of my first novel, *The Breaking of Bumbo*. He came up with Sian Phillips to visit me and that satiric owl, John Bird, my sharer in a grotty flat over the Coffee Pot in Green Street in Cambridge. John appeared later in my film of Bumbo with the divine Joanna Lumley, that peerless beauty. O'Toole sang songs all night in Gaelic, or thereabouts, Sian in Welsh. When a policeman came up the stairs towards dawn to stop us disturbing the peace, O'Toole persuaded him to drink whisky from his helmet and join in the choruses. He always had enough charm to steal the brass off a bobby's badge. I would try to reproduce the scene, when I made the film of *Under Milk Wood*; I had PC Attila Rees pissing into the chamberpot of his headgear, while Dylan's words sounded: "You'll be sorry for that in the morning."

The thing is, to know a star before they become a star. Dylan's extraordinary radio play would never have been shot without O'Toole's commitment. He had played Captain Cat at RADA, the London actors' academy, and he was committed for little pay to the part. He claimed then to have met Elizabeth Taylor; this led to another meeting, while he was playing with Richard Burton in *Becket*; they swapped roles as King and Archbishop. O'Toole said that, after *Cleopatra*, Elizabeth was stalking Richard, wanting a wedding ring. Eddie Fisher, the previous husband, was still pursuing Elizabeth, wanting a reconciliation. All of them were crammed into the back of a limousine, heading from the studio back to London. And O'Toole said, nodding towards the chauffeur, "He is the only one, who hasn't had her." And then he added to me, "I was thrown out of the car, somewhere towards Henley."

Later, Richard Burton told me that one morning, on the set of *Becket*, O'Toole had come in, bearing a whole open bottle of Irish whisky in his hand. He offered it to Burton, who declined and asked what was the particular occasion for celebration.

"It's an Irish birthday," O'Toole said.

"And what day is that?"

"Any day I say it is."

And at that, O'Toole drained the bottle in ten swigs, and fell flat on his back. Shooting resumed twenty-four hours later. Twenty years on, he and Richard asked to see again the film of *Becket*, and Burton, commenting on his own waste of himself, declared, "We want to watch the disintegration of our flesh." Hardly, in the case of O'Toole, who was once asked about what he knew about the many women in his life. "They decide," he said. "We just turn up."

Peter once defined caring for me, in the mode of Samuel Beckett. Sitting opposite him in the buffet in Leeds station were two old tramps, an old man and an old woman. They were sharing one bun and one cup of tea. The man took a bite out of the bun and passed it over to the woman. The woman took a sip of the tea and passed it over to the man, who then took out his false teeth, wiped them on his sleeve, and passed them to the woman, so that she could bite into the bun. "There's compassion," O'Toole said. "True love."

That was the strange quality I was to find in Richard Burton. A capacity to love and to give, but only in excess. His dedication to his craft and sullen art were hid behind the aggression that blistered within his pock-marked face. So he played an early film role, *Look Back in Anger* as a sally at a poor Welsh upbringing, an adoption and many years as an impoverished actor. Now to find himself in the lap of luxury and married to Elizabeth Taylor, who could stand up to him in any fight or drinking bout, he would have to pay tribute to the greatest Welsh bard of all. As he said on arriving on Fishguard Bay railway station to act in *Under Milk Wood*, "I knew Dylan very well and lived with him on and off, but I don't think you can call a genius a friend, and Dylan was unmistakeably a genius. I knew him, shall we say?"

Later he told of an evening spent with Dylan in the Gargoyle Club in Soho. Few were there except for the five-piece band. To Burton, an empty night club was the saddest place on earth and there wasn't a girl in sight.

"Then Dylan started talking about sex. 'What's the sexiest thing you can think of?' he said to me. I said, 'I don't know'. The two of us searched for it in agony. And finally we both agreed that the sexiest thing either of us could think of was blue knickers on a schoolgirl."

That was hardly true now with his tearing passion for Elizabeth Taylor, and their luxury yacht *Kalizma*, containing their four hounds, anchored in the Thames off the Tower of London. They loved their pooches, and because of quarantine regulations, the dogs were not allowed on shore. So I first met Burton in Squire's Mount in Hampstead, hired while Elizabeth was making a film, *Zee & Co.*, of little merit. Believing that he would play the First Voice in *Under Milk Wood*, when he had finished with *Villain*, I was summoned from my house in Regent's Park up north. I would have to pass the star test. Stars would always examine a director, to see whether they would play, how they would play, or would not play at all, at all.

The walls of the redecorated Burton house were hung with apparent Impressionist paintings, an Utrillo and a Modigliani, a Rouault and a Vlaminck. He knew I had been a Cambridge don, and he always claimed he could have been an Oxford intellectual, after his brief RAF stint at Exeter College. He wanted to lord it over me, so he said, "How do you like my Monets and things, Andrew? We have better ones on the yacht." I looked at two or three copies of the real French stuff, and I replied, "Oh, I see. These are only your *travelling* pictures." I got a glint and a grin from him. And then I got the inquisition. "You do know I am the greatest actor in the world, don't you?"

Now if I said, "Yes, you are," I could not direct him. If I said, "No, you are not the greatest actor in the world," he could walk off the film in a huff. But there is always a third answer. So I spread my hands, and I smiled, and I said, "Bleah!" He now laughed. I had passed. We became friends. He even affectionately wrote in his screenplay of Dylan's work, as a leaving present to me, "I have rarely liked or admired a man better!" Flattery, but welcome.

His delivery of words enriched the language, particularly in his reading of *Under Milk Wood*, written for him to play the Second Voice to Dylan Thomas's own First Voice. The Welsh poet's early death gave Burton the leading role in the famous radio version. He told me that Dylan had begged three hundred pounds off him, to avoid the last fatal lecture tour to America. But Burton didn't have the money at the time, although he felt guilty about his refusal thereafter.

He was always conscious of the opportunity in his life, of the help of others, of the love of women, but not of the waste of himself. He was a generous man, dying like Thomas of giving too much to strangers. As a young actor, he was poor. He told me how sad it was at a party to need to court the richest woman in the room, not the most beautiful. Later on, when he was famous, he could choose the most beautiful, and did. In the excess of his nature and the extravagance of his talent, he craved all that love and life could grant to him, from Elizabeth Taylor to the Hollywood style that had ruined so many and made so few.

To work with, he was a supreme professional. His drinking was legendary, but controlled. "I am not drinking on your film," he told me. "That means only one bottle of vodka a day. I am sober on two. But when I am drinking, it is three or more." He was not driven to drink, but used it to escape from melancholy to sociability. Giving so much of himself so often, he needed the stimulus. Yet his genius was more than the infinite capacity for imbibing shots. It lay in a voice that seemed to contain all the passion and powers, wearinesses and weaknesses of our kind. To hear him speak was to listen to the human condition.

He always seemed to me like the Scots doctor in the Border legend. The doctor dreams of meeting the Faery Queen. One night, walking on the moors, he does. The Queen falls in love with him and snatches him away to join her glittering court and live in a world of fantasy. The doctor forgets his trade. One day, the Queen tires of him. He returns to Edinburgh, an older man, unable to practise his calling, forever longing for what he has lost and never really wanted.

If Burton seemed to squander his great talents, it was from an expanse of spirit. His Shakespearean roles remain in the memory as equal to those of Laurence Olivier and John Gielgud. He told me of his Jenkins brothers from Wales, visiting him at the Old Vic, and saying, "Give us the long words, Richard." And he would say, "The multitudinous seas incarnadine, making the green one red." Then his family would fall on the dressing-room floor in fond laughter.

For all his love of Dylan, Richard never meant to make my film. "You have to schedule me back one week," Peter O'Toole said to me. "I have to prepare my part. I never thought the film would happen. Richard Burton never meant to play. But you fixed it so he had to. The greatest actor of Wales going back home to appear in the greatest Welsh bard's greatest work. And four television crews waiting to cover him shooting. He had to go. You're a clever bastard, fixing all that publicity."

I had fixed nothing at all. In fact, I wanted minimal publicity and no television crews covering the shooting. We had far too little time as it was. Already a miracle, getting the three biggest stars in the world to agree to play in *Under Milk Wood* for a mere ten thousand pounds apiece. For I had the shock of my life, when I had a call in the basement of my Nash terrace house in Regent's Park. It was O'Toole's agent and partner, the expressive Jules Buck.

"Andrew," he swore, "you're a lucky bastard. You haven't got the two biggest stars in the world, you've got all three."

I swallowed.

"Not Miss Taylor," I said.

"Yes. Elizabeth too."

"But what bloody part? It's Under Milk Wood. She's not Welsh."

"Your problem. You've got her. Or no picture."

"Rosie Probert," I said. "The sailors' whore. Burton would agree with that."

"Sure. Anything. Short shoot. And she can't travel. Bad back."

"But we're shooting in Wales."

"For Wales," Buck said, "read Pinewood. Luxury trailer too. And costume choice."

I put down the receiver, knowing my fate. And it was to be worked out at a meeting in the offices of the National Film Finance Corporation off Soho Square, where I had once had my first London garret flat. The scenario seemed to come from *The Producers*, the funniest film ever to be made about theatrical finance. Not always about how many bums on paying seats, but also about not paying taxes or backers.

I had always liked the NFFC Chairman, the genial John Terry, who had treated my youth and inexperience with hope and respect. He had also raised a third of the small budget of £300,000 for the first time from a Merchant Bank, Hill Samuel – the wife of the head man was Welsh herself. Jules Buck was there for O'Toole, also the representative of Burton and Taylor, the urbane Hugh French, dressed in the retired colonel mode. I chose to come to this cabal without a lawyer. I was shielded only by my expectations and my ignorance. What I remember of the debate was a discussion about the profits of the film, if there were to be any.

"For O'Toole," Buck announced, "I'll take fifty per cent."

"For my two stars," French demanded. "Fifty per cent for Elizabeth. And fifty per cent for Richard."

"And fifty per cent for the money," Terry added.

I could just about add it up. As in *The Producers*, two hundred per cent. And nothing for me. I rose to my feet.

"Gentlemen," I said, "I can count. Two hundred per cent. You work it out without me. I will go to gaol if necessary. But we will make Under Milk Wood. And I will sign any document for my company Timon Films, which has the rights. Just put it in front of me."

And so I left the room. As each of the three stars was making a million dollars a picture, I couldn't work out why the big trio would appear in *Under Milk Wood* for only £10,000 per person – my own wages – set against the completion of the film. Could it be for the love of Dylan, as it was for me? Rather doubtful.

Anyway, a contract was rushed to me, which I signed. The odd thing was that the media copyrights in *Under Milk Wood* were assigned to Timon Films. Buck and his associates, however, took over all distribution through a company registered in the Bahamas. I didn't care. We had to get on with making the picture and there were only a few weeks to go, because of the schedule of Richard and Elizabeth in their galactic stay in Squire's Mount and on their yacht moored off the Tower of London. Of course, I should have known better or worse, but I never did. Reckless as

I was, people always said of me that I wanted to make the movie too much. I did not consider the fact that he who sells the film and collects the takings can ensure that he and his clients get their share. Others may not.

From my reputation, Elizabeth Taylor disliked me on sight. She felt undereducated, her husband had wanted to become a don, and I had been an academic. In her opulent and booze-stocked Shepperton studio dressing-room, while making her previous film, *Zee and Co.*, she appeared somewhat dishevelled, if that was possible. She gave me three orders. Firstly, her back was too bad to take the train to Wales; I would have to film her two-day shoot in London. Secondly, it had to be at the end of the schedule, as her movie was a long way from a wrap. And although she was only playing the small part of a Welsh whore called Rosie Probert, she would require three Parisian nightdresses, at the cost of six hundred pounds – half of our total costume budget.

The next time I met her was the *coup-de-grâce*. Richard had invited myself and the comic Ryan Davies, who played the Second Voice, for a drunken evening in his Camden house. After a few bottles, Richard decided we were his two best friends, and he presented each of us with a silver goblet, given by the Rotary clubs of Wales in grateful memory to their favourite son and daughter, Elizabeth and Richard Burton, *alias* Jenkins. "I have to cut all the jewellery advertisements out of the glossy magazines," Richard was confiding in us, "or I would be ruined. She loves the rocks."

He was unable, however, to forestall the apparition that burst through the door – Elizabeth, in a yellow hot-pants wool suit, covered by a wild mink coat, the tails of the little beasts twirling on the floor. "Taraah!", she cried, and then she saw the silverware in the hands of Ryan and me. "What are you doing with *my* goblet?" Elizabeth screeched in the tones of the Three Bears, objecting to Goldilocks. I handed one silver cup back to Richard, Ryan handed him the other, and we left hotfoot into the London night. Behind us, a voice like a police siren rent the black air.

Except for her magical violet eyes and ruby lips, Elizabeth Taylor was far from being the most beautiful woman in the world. "Absolute nonsense," Richard Burton said of his wife. "She has a double chin, an overdeveloped chest, and she's rather short in the leg." That was why she always travelled with her own personal photographer, Gianni Bozzachi, and his wife Claudye, a hairdresser. The snapper would fling himself on the ground to get a worm's eye view of the star, while shooting upwards. This made her seem tall and slender, without an extra chin. Her face was smaller, but Claudye always made a black halo of bouffant dark hair, so that the head was in proportion to the whole body. Elizabeth was an expert on her own best effect.

When the three stars had finally signed their non-committal two paragraphs each, stating that they might well turn up to make the film, and the money began to flow, I found that Elizabeth would only play for two days, Richard for five-and-a-half days, and Peter O'Toole for five. And time was very short, given our schedule. Only three weeks to prepare to rebuild and equip Lower Fishguard. I could never have done that without one of the most remarkable women I have ever met, Jacquemine Charrott-Lodwidge. A Celt from Britanny and Cornwall, she had been a double agent for the British and Vichy in the Near East in the Second World War. She had even possessed a jealous leopard in Egypt, which would leap on her lover's back with its claws to stimulate his drive. For years, she had been my fixer in my huge empty house in Regent's Park, then my location finder and props manager on *Under Milk Wood*. She could find anything and trade well. Her only defect was that she had one eye and drove her sports car very fast.

With an excellent designer Geoffrey Tozer, we built false fronts on the dock cottages and constructed a whole whaler's ship side on the first floor of Captain Cat's home. Quay Street was transformed into Cockle Row, and five stone cottages at Glyn-y-mel were transformed into a town square around a village pump. The *pièce-de-resistance* was to create in front of the public lavatories the undertaker's parlour of Evans the Death. So all seemed well. Though my production company Timon Films was fully liable for everything, I knew or thought I knew that Richard Burton was coming back to Wales for the first time in ten years, and all the press and television was waiting for him.

And come he did, because they were waiting for him. He could not disappoint them. He could never raise his head in Wales again, if he did not go, because everyone knew he was coming. Yet it was not my doing. It was the doing of his own publicity machine. And by the time he thought he might back out, it was too late. His publicity made him appear. He was hoist by his own PR, not mine.

He did put me to one final test. He had arrived in Fishguard at four o'clock in the afternoon. I begged him to appear by the dockside to perform the opening sequence, coming from the sea during the ten minutes of twilight, when the dusk can be shot. The whole crew was there, examining the credentials of an untried young director. Driven by the Basque chauffeur Gaston, the vast black Burton Rolls Royce, equipped with a television set and a full bar, arrived near the set. The back seat was empty. Richard Burton was indisposed. My film looked like being over before it began. With forty experienced pairs of eyes as gimlets on my back, I walked forward and considered the sea. Then I turned and said, "Same place. Time. Eight o'clock tomorrow morning." Then I walked off. And so, all might begin, however unlikely that was.

Andrew Sinclair with Peter O'Toole.

Andrew Sinclair with Elizabeth Taylor.

Andrew Sinclair with Richard Burton
in the film of *Under Milk Wood*.

Elizabeth Taylor and Peter O'Toole.

Elizabeth Taylor at last with pennies on her eyes.

THE MAKING

I had worn a black tight leather coat for years. Not that I was a biker, but I wished to unsettle any stranger who might approach me. To this, Jacquemine Charrott-Lodwidge added a leather skull-cap with a chinstrap, as worn by fighter pilots in the First World War. This gear gave me a semblance of authority.

I had also decided upon a three-weather alternative schedule. The whole crew had to fall in at 8 AM outside my home on set – the false pub, *The Sailor's Arms*, on the quayside. I looked at the sky in the early morning, and so I earned the name of Andrew the Luck. Regularly, the clouds in their quilts across Wales only parted above Fishguard and its bay. Indeed, the transatlantic airliners would use the town as a marker in their descent towards Heathrow. There had to be a hayfield sun in March, a blessing not seen in thirty years. "*Wales* in winter!" said the drenched warriors streaming home from Polanski's blasted *Macbeth*. "Jesus! Not only did Banquo blow off his horse, but the bloody horse blew away too."

So given sun or cloud or rain, I would change the shooting order to every condition. Our stand-by was a deserted Rank stone flour store, which provided us with a dozen small sets, even with a tempest outside. We worked on the run, with the heavies from Lee Electrics humping the Brute lights and tracks and Mitchell camera equipment as if these were as light as mortars or machine-guns. Most of them had been in the armed forces, and a film crew on location is a pirate raid. I knew their reputation well enough to ask them to remove the eyesore in my main period set on the dock, a concrete lamp-post that defiled the sea view.

"How much to lose that?," I asked the Jake, the head gaffer.

"Four bottles of whisky, guv."

"Done."

The next morning, the excrescence had vanished, as though it had never been there. And nobody seemed to notice or to care. I did not know then that the Lee Brothers had also rewired all the digs except *The Sailors' Arms*, so as to save the energy bills on the budget. Raiders, indeed. And as for the four bottles of whisky, alas, I would have to deal with them later.

Two other tricks I had learned from the old lags in the film trade. The first was the essential bit of dingle – in my case, two pieces, a flowering plastic cherry tree and a blossoming yellow gorse-bush. As we were shooting in March in a Welsh winter, whenever the blooming plants were seen, one might believe all was happening in the required spring. That was when those real buds burst out. And the dingle also blocked the sight of the ferryboat crossing to Dublin, or whatever intruded on a good angle.

The other wheeze was the moveable cornerpiece. End the Action with the actor moving from the chosen set, Cut and shift the set to wherever, start shooting it and Pull Back to the actor moving in, and Bingo! The player was transported from Piccadilly to Timbuctoo as though he or she had just turned the corner. Our ticket to four different graveyards was to start on the tomb of NORMA JANE, the wartime romance of the Two Voices. Anyway, because Elizabeth Taylor could not come to the Welsh cemetery, and Richard Burton's short schedule did not allow it, we had to bring a cemetery to them.

We only had a forty days' budget about as fat as Our Lord's, when He had the same schedule in the wilderness. What with sixty sets and seventy actors, we had to spend a quarter of our time just shifting from scene to scene. Everything and everyone had to work too well, beyond normal and halfway to dream. The technicians would mutter, and I would answer, "Miracles happen daily." Frankly they had to, so they did.

My shooting script for *Under Milk Wood* had blank pages opposite those marking the list of shots. On them, I drew patterns worthy of Euclid and geometry. As Richard Burton had recorded the First Voice in advance, the timing of each shot had to coincide to a second on the flow of his speech. Also the stars were never at Fishguard at the same time, but they had to appear just so. And finally, I knew I would lose the magical ripple of Dylan's writing by cutting. Each little scene had to dissolve on movement into the other to cosset the stream of the poetic words. Then the audience would not wonder, any more than author had, whether the actors were living or dead, awake or lost in a dream. How could I interrupt such a sinuous incantation?

And so a reporter heard me say, while having a snippet of Elizabeth Taylor's recording played on tape, as she dumped herself into the part of Rose Probert, flat on her back. I timed the length of her Voice Over off a tracking camera. Then I said:

"Thirty-six and a half seconds." *Pause.* "Settle, please." *Silence.* "Turn over. *The camera started running.* "Action."

Elizabeth lies still, holding her breath.
"*Knock twice, Jack*" – it is Rosie's voice –

"At the door of my grave
And ask for Rosie."

It is Rosie's voice but it is not coming from Rosie. Her mouth and eyes fly open and Elizabeth shrieks: "Oh, turn that OFF!"

Mr Sinclair: "*CUT.*"

A second silence.

Mr Sinclair: "We've got to tie it …"

Elizabeth (*a shout*): "Oh, shit!"

Mr Sinclair: "We've got to …"

Elizabeth: "Well couldn't you *tell* me? I don't particularly *like* hearing my own voice."

It is a recording of what we will at this point hear on the sound track. Mr Sinclair approaches Elizabeth and speaks in a low voice. Then he says to the Sound Engineer: "Turn it down." Then: "Action."

The scene is filmed, the taped voice soft, Elizabeth again holding her breath, and closing her eyes.

I then made my only Alfred Hitchcock appearance in my film. Wearing my black leather gloves, I picked two odd pennies from a convenient saucer and placed the copper coins over her closed lids. That was once the burial custom in Wales. Only my gloves appeared. But did I wish a moribund Elizabeth? Perish the thought. She let out a big breath at the end of the take.

"Cut," I said, withdrawing my hands. "Print that. And Elizabeth, when you can manage it, could you please lie stone still again for your next Voice Over as Rosie Probert?" And she did too:

> "Remember her.
> She is forgetting.
> The earth which filled her mouth
> Is vanishing from her.
> Remember me.
> I have forgotten you.
> I am going into the darkness of the darkness for ever.
> I have forgotten that I was ever born."

The lines I kept on remembering were in the remark that Cassius spoke to me, when I was playing Brutus in *Julius Caesar* on the Eton stage. In his memoirs, Ferdie Mount wrote that I looked even as a youth like the savage mask of that Roman hero, done by Michelangelo. However that was, it had taken me a long time to grow old enough to fit into my face. And what did Shakespeare say?

> *Men at some time are masters of their fate.*
> *The fault, dear Brutus, is not in our stars*
> *But in ourselves, that we are underlings.*

That was too true. However difficult Richard and Elizabeth were, the fault was in me, if I could not make the film work, even by drawing diagrams of the constellations on the blank page in order to align the movements of the stars with their prerecorded voice patterns. Yes, they had both been too drunk for me to rely on them getting Dylan's words perfect on each take. Yet they would still mime their parts and entrance the world.

This device of a drifting camera gave a unity to the film, a visual reason for all the marvellous speeches of the Voices, that orchestration of words which makes *Under Milk Wood* as binding as a spell. But it did not solve the problem of the final coming together of the townspeople, nor did it help the dying fall of the picture, which trailed away into nothing. But we do not always make movies. Sometimes movies make us.

We were filming the night shot of Evans the Death, the undertaker, asleep by an open coffin, laughing in his dreams. The undertaker's shop had been built by us in front of two lavatories on the quayside of Lower Fishguard, which otherwise served naturally as Cockle Row. We had set up the shot through the window of the shop on the first three letters FUN from FUNERALS – beyond the glass, the end of the bed, with Evans the Death's toes curling through a hole in his purple socks.

Then a coastguard siren wailed behind us, meaning trouble at sea. And policemen hurried up the quayside, and we stopped work, and a boat set out across the bay. And we looked at the cliffs opposite until the boat came back. In it, the body of a drowned boy. One of our electricians thought it was the body of his child, and he broke down. The boy turned out to be the child of a local freelance cameraman, who normally worked for television. But in the dead child, we all saw our own deaths and the deaths of our children. So we packed up and went home till the morning.

The funeral was two days later. So I and the Associate Producer left the scene of Polly Garter singing, "Little Willy Wee is dead, dead, dead…", to pay our respects to the family of the boy and leave wreaths from the company. The father met us, a brave and good man. He said he would not find it easy to leave overnight his wife and other children and his home for some weeks now. So we offered him work in getting us some shots of seals, which we might need. For he knew where the seals were at this time of year. What we did not know was that the seals lay at the bottom of a thousand foot cliff. Putting his Arriflex on his back, the courageous cameraman and two of our party got down that cliff, risking their lives and losing the top of a finger. The father came back with some spectacular shots, including one of a group of seals humping away into the foam.

We went back next week and did the shot of the undertaker laughing by the coffin, although nobody wanted to think of it. Dylan had written it, and it still had to be done. But when I saw the rushes of the seals and I re-read *Under Milk Wood* for the hundredth time, I saw where the magic and the end of the picture lay. Celtic myths are full of seals coming back from the sea; their singing voices are meant to be the drowned dead, like the five sailors who come back to Captain Cat in his dreams. "I lost my step in Nantucket," says Dancing Williams, now down salt deep into the Davy dark. And endlessly, Dylan refers to dreams coming from the black sea :

> *"Only you can hear and see, behind the eyes of the sleepers, the ... flight and fall and despairs and big seas of their dreams...."*
> *"Now behind the eyes and secrets of the dreamers in the streets rocked to sleep by the sea, see the ... wrecks and sprats and shells and fishbones, whalejuice and moonshine and small salt fry dished up by the hidden sea."*

So I filmed a night dream dance in the pouring rain, with a gale blowing the roofs away, while the actors playing the people of Llaregyb caracoled around the town pump and pranced away into the waves, and they were dissolved into seals, and Satan's jester walked back from the wild drowned caper he had led from the back of a squealing pig to the black Milk Wood, where the Satan of Richard Burton was waiting, crossing himself and smiling darkly, with his last incantation sounding, that begins:

> *"The Wood, whose every tree – foot's cloven in the black glad sight of the hunters of lovers ..."*

And so the film had an end, a magical end, that had grown out of its words and its making, out of the life of the welcoming town and the death of the boy that had its sad meaning to us all, out of the rich deep words of the Welsh poet of poets and the tears in Captain Cat's eyes as he remembers Rosie Probert and his lost sailoring days:

> *"Seas barking like seals,*
> *Blue seas and green,*
> *Seas covered with eels*
> *And mermen and whales."*

Richard Burton had said to me that Dylan's play was all about religion, sex and death, and I did not understand his words until the film was over.

My preacher and teacher was not the fond-foolish Reverend Eli Jenkins nor the dark Puritan Jack Black from Dylan's text, but my dandy-dark cameraman Bob Huke, who made me watch the twilights away in his quest for that one shot at evening which he called "the magic hour." And in that "dusk and ceremonial dust, and night's first darkening snow," I sensed the timeless powers of the Gwaun Valley, where the pagan stones still stand at the doorways and the mistletoe hangs from the wind-bent oaks, the powers of light and night, wind and water, stone and hill, crow and cromlech, Celtic cross and bleeding yew, which are still the old gods in that Pembrokeshire where the ancient Celts quarried blue rocks to drag all the way to Stonehenge. And I knew that we only had to resign ourselves to the place and its doings to recapture the spell of Dylan's words and describe Milk waking Wood. We were all the servants of the dead Dylan Thomas, who caught the essence of all Welsh sea-towns and made an incantation of them.

In his love of his part, Peter O'Toole even briefly gave up the drink because he might lose his sight. As the ultimate professional, which he was, he insisted on wearing milky-blue contact lenses that covered both of his eye-balls to play the blind Captain Cat. The trouble was that he could only stand the lenses in his eyes for half-an-hour at a whack, and then he was really going blind after four days of it. If he had not been such a superb performer, capable of five-minute takes hitting an unseen mark without a wrong word, we could never have completed the shots on him without his sight. As it was, the courage of the man lasted far beyond the good of his eyes until the last four longish shots, which we took from the back or with his lids closed.

Any evening that his performing was over in Wales, Peter led the riotous nightly singing and dancing at the bar of the Fishguard Bay Hotel. He insisted that the ditty was *The Cuckoo Song*. In the middle of a line of a dozen cavorting grave men, who had all dropped their trousers, he high-kicked and belted out the words like a *soubrette*. The spotless Associate Producer John Comfort wore white underpants, the hairdresser Ramon wore blue ones, with two Lee Brothers in striped and red flag knickers. On O'Toole's orders, anyone who laughed was thrown out and had to buy a round for everybody. That was his game, as I would have mine.

The thing about the sixty-five or so Welsh actors was they that were all natural players. But most of them had never appeared in a film before. As Richard Burton told me in a rare moment of self-deprecation, "All the

Welsh are actors, and I am one of the worst of them. That is why I am a professional." In fact, because he was a professional, he would only ask for the size of the lens and his movements, and then he would give a performance no larger than would suit the camera. In close-up, he never blinked or showed emotion. Only his eyes stared, as if he were a hypnotist. Most of the other Welsh players overacted, as they did in real life. I had to tell them to do little or nothing. As I used to explain:

"In a close-up, a wink or a twitch looks like an invitation to a bed or a hanging. In medium shot, do what you do normally, but less so. And in a long shot, you can stand on your hands naked. Because if something interesting is happening in front, nobody will notice you."

The art of the cinema lies in underacting and murmuring. On the stage, the drama demands gestures and throwing your voice to the back of the stalls and up to the gods. In the poetic flow of the phrases in *Under Milk Wood*, we had to strike a balance in performance between real life in a fishing village and the flowering magnificence of Dylan's prose.

Summoned back to London and Lee Studios because of Elizabeth's bad back, we had to wait all morning for her to appear. We only had two days to shoot her. For if she and Richard did not leave British shores by tomorrow midnight, their back taxes would have settled much of the National Debt. I went to her dressing-room, and I put down a costly gold Egyptian serpent bracelet, as a peace offering from my pocket. Unfortunately, she was making up herself as Cleopatra, all *kohl* and rouge and peacock eyelids. "That won't do," I heard myself daring to say. "You're a Welsh sailor's whore of the 'fifties. You can't look like that."

"I always look like Cleopatra," she said, and dismissed me.

She did not come on set until noon. I decided to turn her into Captain Cat's wet dream, as in the text. "Grease the lens," I told my cameraman, Bob Huke, who asked, "Do I make her look beautiful, or like the back end of a bus?" I swallowed and gulped out, "Beautiful, please. She has picture approval."

We laid her on the brass bed and bunged in three shots before lunch on the incredible violet eyes. I noticed that Bob was performing in front of the Brute lights, as the conductor of an orchestra. Only his baton was a black ruler. When she was gone, I asked Bob what he was doing. "Hiding her three chins," he said, "even when she moves. The thingy throws a shadow across her neck. We call it a Charliebar. Any Charlie can use it."

He used it with such skill that Elizabeth never looked more beautiful on her unwilled brass bed.

Peter O'Toole now saved the picture, when he popped his head round the door of my Lee Studio room to find me slumped in despair over the debacle in the morning.

"You've lost your fillum, Andrew," he said. "Liz is not appearing after lunch. But – for what I am about to do for you, I deserve the Victoria Cross and bloody Bar." He then disappeared. After a long and boozy lunch at the Paesana in Bayswater, he and Burton, who liked me and had coached her, held her up between their shoulders while she read off her lines. And the consummate O'Toole, who always told me "Get this shot," when he did something unexpected, conjured a real laugh out of that immaculate and uncreasable face.

Playing Captain Cat as a young sailor, he leapt into bed with her, and hitched up his shirt. Tattooed in biro on his tummy was, *I Love You, Rosie Probert,* the part she was playing. She collapsed in a gale of mirth. She wasn't aware, I wasn't told, the result, a miracle of spontaneity. She left without saying good-bye to me, although she did write in Burton's screenplay, which he gave to me, that it had been a fantastic experience. Indeed, for both of us.

I had nearly lost Pat Kavanagh, too. For her love scene as Norma Jane with Richard Burton and Ryan Davies, a straw-strewn floor in a stone barn had been set up. While she was snogging passionately in her flesh-coloured slip with Richard, I heard him murmuring to her. Would she come to Puerto Vallarta to see more of him? That was too much for me. I leant forward, picked up a stiff straw, and scratched the sole of her bare foot with its tip. She glanced at me and away from Richard. She got the point. And she never went to Mexico.

There is an abyss between actors chatting off set and film crews. Actors are forever talking about how well they played their last part. They were a great success, even if the production was dire. Film crews are different. They only tell disaster stories. What a dreadful thing happened to me on the way to making a movie! The lights blew, the producer skipped, the money was as liquid as a running sewer, the egg-and-bacon butties were stone cold, there was no booze in Arabia except fermented camel milk, *etcetera*. What was common to all was that the director was an arsehole. And that, for a young director like me, was the challenge. How could I earn their RESPECT?

Everyone among the film technicians thought I was barmy. But I was the producer, the director, the screen-writer and most important – the money. And they were getting paid due to the brilliant organisation of my Associate Producer John Comfort, and Maureen, his lynx-like wife. As for the crew, they had never seen a film made in this way, by a camera rocking and swooping to a timing in seconds, dashing in and out of shot quicker than a minnow fleeing from a pike.

"Come in slow, Dennis," I'd say to my Camera Operator, "on left top corner of frame. Hold for eight seconds on the single line of Waldo's Mother. Then come down quick in centre frame. And we'll cut."

This was gobbledegook to the crew. I could never put the picture together. But even if it turned out to be an inevitable and unreleased turkey, their wages were sent to the bank weekly. Mutiny was out of the question. So what the hell! Do as the mad guvnor says, grab the take, and bitch about him on the next picture.

Secretly, I was rough-cutting with my adept editor Willy Kemplen on Sundays. His father had sliced up the rushes on *The Third Man*, and he claimed to have recorded in an Austrian café and brought to David Lean the famous Karas zither theme tune. I was now working non-stop for sixteen hours a day for the seven weeks of shooting. But there could be only one way of cutting. So on the last evening before the wrap, I would show these seasoned disaster merchants how the film did splice together in spite of all its feints and lunges in a weird and wonderful maze of shooting, all short takes and darting lenses as logical as a labyrinth.

Most of the crew changed their predetermined minds. And then Andrew the Luck pulled his great coup in the last shots of the boats rocking in the bay. He would even earn the respect of the Lee mob. Worrying and working day and night in my hidey-hole and avoiding the endless nocturnal drinking and singing at the local hotels, 1 had been summoned by Jake, the leader of the Lee Electric gang, who had lost the concrete lamp-post.

"Governor," he said, "we're drinking the four bottles of Scotch you gave us. You got to pay and have one on us. OK?"

I nodded again. And in the Wild Welsh West of Pembrokeshire, the Lee boys set up four rummers of whisky side by side on the bar. I knocked them down in ten minutes, the one after t'other, and I drove straight back, before I tumbled down myself. For I had to rise at the crack of dawn, if it cracked at all, or even inched up.

On the last day of the movie, we were filming the opening sequence, the fishing boats bobbing in the harbour, a day-for-night shot. The Grand National was also running and jumping. There was heavy betting on the race with the local bookie. I'd had a walkout long ago with a horsey debutante, who married a jockey, who had won the Grand National and become a trainer and gone demented. He had bought her a horse called Specify, which had been a flat-racer, went lame, and took on the fences on three sound legs. The odds were 38-1, and I laid twenty quid on it to win. The crew fell about in laughter. Only the clapper-boy backed my hunch. Sixth over the last fence, Specify sprinted in first. A holy hush fell over the set.

"Andrew the Luck again," I said. "A party tonight on me. But you'll have to play the Governor's Game. Because I can dance and spin faster than you can drink."

Talk about trial by exploit and idiocy, *macho* as *tonto*. I could whirl with the best, a trick I had learned while dancing Scots reels. And as far as alcohol, it took a wee while to fuddle. So my rules were:

- Down one short Scotch and spin ten times in one minute.
- Repeat every minute.
- The last man wins.
- The prize. Elizabeth Taylor's garter, as worn by Rosie Probert in the film.

We had quite enough to drink, before my game began. A jig was struck up by the local strummers, and twenty players took to the floor. I swigged and twirled, the ceiling twisting above my head. Oblivious of the others, I glugged and pirouetted nine, ten, eleven, a dozen times – and I crashed down on my thirteenth manoeuvre. Jake had been on the whirl almost as much as me, but he had staggered off a turn before. Unconscious, I was carried off, crowned by Elizabeth's garter as a laurel wreath across my brow.

I woke in hell and sickness, four hours later. My dear Associate John Comfort had sat up with me, to see that I did not choke on my own vomit. Still besotted by this trial of strength, I told him to carry me into the rushes of the last day of shooting, even if it killed me. I had to show the crew and the technicians who was boss. And so it was, the stupid struggle for male supremacy in movies.

Not quite a living being, I lurched into the morning showing, and I earned respect. To the Lee boys, I became something of a legend. When I would meet them on later sets, they would smile and say: "You were the only bugger who ever got Jake down."

And myself, too.

Andrew Sinclair with Peter O'Toole.

Richard Burton with Pat Kavanagh as Norma Jane.

Peter O'Toole as blind Captain Cat.

Pat Kavanagh and Richard Burton.

Elizabeth Taylor records her role with Peter O'Toole.

David Jason with Ruth Madoc.

David Jason with Meg Wynn Owen.

Victor Spinetti with the mermaid Glynis Johns.

Ryan Davies rides a boar.

HANGOVER

Under Milk Wood was one of the more impossible films to make, and I doubt that I will ever put that sort of thing together again. There really would have been no way of making the movie except for two great strokes of luck regarding casting. First of all, Dylan Thomas had originally written the play for himself and Richard Burton, and Richard had always wanted to do the First Voice. Second, Peter O'Toole had first played Captain Cat when he was a drama student. Peter and I had been students together, and I think stars only really trust you if they've known you when you were both poor and unknown. I gave the screenplay to O'Toole and he said he would do it. Then when Richard heard that O'Toole was in, he said that he, too, would do it, and furthermore his wife then (Elizabeth Taylor) would take the Rosie Probert role. All three were willing to work for small fees and large percentages. After that, of course, it was relatively simple to get the necessary funds.

All the actors were excellent. Many of the professional actors were from Cardiff television and had never been on film before, but they had a marvellous quality of performance: all you had to do as a director was bring *down* their performance. If you ever dealt with professional actors – particularly the Welsh – you know they are always playing over the top with exaggerated gestures. You must continually say, "Quiet, quiet, do *nothing*." Once they do nothing, they are acting very well. All the extras in the film are just local Fishguard people. Even the children are exactly what they seem to be: they sing like that naturally. As the Reverend Eli Jenkins says: "Praise the Lord! We are a musical nation."

Many of the militant Welsh think of Dylan Thomas as a sort of Welsh Uncle Tom – a stereotype of the Welsh people, recognizable everywhere. I think he did embody the inbred contradiction of the Welsh. On the one hand, there is a Wales which is terribly puritan and middle-class and then, right beside it, there is a strong, lusty old tradition of boozing and thieving and roistering about. And the Welsh have never put them together. In Lower Fishguard, I found that up the hill lived the middle classes (Mrs Ogmore Pritchard's spiritual relatives, you could say), but down the hill was a bawdy village where in fact one woman was having an affair with the undertaker and everyone was waiting to see what would happen when her husband changed shifts or came home early some day. When we first arrived there was great disapproval by the middle classes. Respectable people kept saying, "You can't shoot down there; they're swapping wives all over the place." But when we left, the villagers wept and sang hymns.

Nonetheless, there were great technical problems. First there were Dylan's marvellous words to contend with. The language is so rich and powerful that it's spellbinding. I had always thought words like that were a form of orchestra, that they could substitute for music. Actually I found that Dylan had written 400 little scenes, which would have meant constant cutting – chop, chop, chop – and you cannot have hundreds of short little chopped up bits with the words going across and still serve a dead genius' work. You should try to make the visual rhythms respond to the flow of the language to a certain extent. So although we were shooting out of sequence and sometimes even a month apart, I would tell the cameraman to drift the camera out at 80 degrees on the top left-hand edge. He would say, "but you can't cut it together," and I would say, "but it's the only way." There were no cover shots or anything like that, we would just drift the camera out and I would make a diagram, and then a month later we would drift it in at pretty much the same angle and that would be that. It was carefully planned with all those drifting cameras, which is a concept taken from the elder Ophuls in his film on Lola Montes.

There were usually only three takes, and the final film has only about three minutes cut out. There was no waste at all, it was planned to that degree. Actually there was a great advantage in this: if you only shoot something one way, then that's the way it's shot and they can't do anything about it; there's no possible chance for substitution. It also accelerates your shooting time. Officially we shot *Under Milk Wood* in forty days, but twelve of those were spent moving, so it was actually only twenty-eight days.

Of course, there are other poetic things in the film besides the language, such as the camerawork. Bob Huke, the cameraman, did a film,

The Virgin and the Gypsy, which was shot entirely through thin gauze. This is an old trick which takes the sharp edges off everything, and I used it throughout *Under Milk Wood* as well. We also did some day-for-night shots in the sunlight by photographing through heavy gauze. Also, I gave every character a distinct colour – the Pughs were always in brown, Captain Cat is in greys and blues – and this produces a strange beauty because there is always one dominant colour.

Many of the thorniest problems had to be solved before we ever shot a foot of film. Dylan was brought up in the great tradition of the British documentary. He was a screenwriter himself and wrote one and a half good screenplays and several bad ones. In the heyday of radio in the forties, you could put Winston Churchill on the air and everyone knew who it was; you didn't have to explain. I think Dylan got the technique of Two Voices from that. But in a screenplay, it's no good. I had two choices. I could have used unexplained voices off on the side commenting on the action, but that would have worked only for a documentary, not for something like *Under Milk Wood.* Or you can say, as I did, well, just who ARE these voices? Who are the two men? Why do they come into the village, how can they conjure up dreams, what are they doing there, why do they leave? Dylan Thomas explains none of this. There are just Two Voices. We don't know who they are, what their relationship to the town is, nothing at all.

Fortunately I was very familiar with Dylan's life and writings. I knew his first sexual experience was with a red-haired girl who switched beds with him and a friend for a whole weekend. Dylan referred to the experience all his life in various stories: he was always hung up on one woman with two or three men. And that's what you see in the film: Polly Garter reminiscing about her dead lovers ("Tom, Dick and Harry were three fine men / And I'll never have such loving again I..."), children playing kissing games. Sinbad Sailors pining after Gossamer Beynon, and of course the two men with the girl in the khaki pantsuit – all four versions of love going on in that hot afternoon. And I think it true to Dylan's intention.

I am the one who thinks that these two men (the Two Voices) are dead and that they come back and go through these old rites. But they are not just human beings. On another level they are the Devil and his Disciple. And I carefully introduced all this mingling of fancy and reality to the audience gradually. The film deliberately starts in a very pedestrian way because many people haven't been to Wales and it's for a world audience. When the text talks about "cats … on the one cloud of the roofs" in the opening sequence, you see two cats on a cloudy roof. You might think Dylan was being poetic, but the Welsh caulk their roofs with lime, so it's really a literal description. This sort of prosaic beginning is a Hitchcock trick to hook the audience into thinking that all this is literal, actual reality. Then as the film goes on, the 'unreal' things come in bit by bit and no one really minds that this is the devil and his disciple wandering through the town: the dead and the living together. Finally you end up with the pure magic of the final scenes with the dancing people round the village pump dissolved into seals.

I have been criticised both ways about this reality / magic mixture. Some people wonder why at first it is just like an illustration of the text. Well, it is in the beginning, and quite deliberately so. But by the end, it is so far away that I have been equally criticised for putting in the dream sequences and using all the images from Celtic legends.

Of course, I had to decide at the outset that I was, in fact, dealing with a magical piece of work. Dylan originally did not distinguish the living from the dead in his voices. The question was, do you give all the dead green rotting faces and some semblance of being 'really' dead and bring them back as spooks? Or do you make them just like the living? You see them and it doesn't matter whether they are dead or alive. I'm Scotch-Irish and very Celtic in my thinking. I see dead people and there is no problem about it: they just appear and then they go away again. And there are too many instances of the dead turning up to visit – particularly in the Welsh regions – for anyone to bother worrying about it. People in that part of the world do believe they will encounter the dead and that the seals are indeed the drowned dead. The old pagan legends remain. The people of the Gwaun Valley where we shot *Under Milk Wood* still celebrate Saturnalia every Twelfth Night. Circles of standing stones, probably used by the Druids for worship, still exist in the countryside. Old phallic stones still stand in front of every door just as they have for thousands of years. It seemed impossible to ignore the magic.

I still hadn't solved the problem of the ending for the film, but I began thinking, "Just who ARE these village people?" I went back to the old Celtic legends and found that, in them, the seals are always the drowned dead; they come out of the sea from the drowned sailors. Then I started thinking about the sea: the sailors coming from the sea to shore drifting over "the sea-dark streets," the drift of the sea and the moving camera which was producing a gliding, wave-like motion from shot to shot, then the dead boy coming drowned from the sea as we shot the funeral scene – and it all began to fit. I suddenly saw the seals – the drowned dead – coming in from the sea into the town. I used other old legends like the devil (which sometimes meant a pagan priest) and his disciple, the dancing round the maypole, and a sort of pied piper leading to the seals. It solved the problem of the film, and in a way the death of the boy became meaningful.

Although the film was carefully planned and *we* made *it*, in other ways *it* made *us*. When I say it was a very strange film, I mean that it was not quite within our control. Technically, yes; but rationally, absolutely not. The final sequence, which had been prompted by such strange happenings, was shot at night in a howling force-four gale. The rain was coming down so fast that the cameraman said it would be all right – it was too fast to register on the film (and it didn't).

We were manning the lights and everyone was singing and boozing until five in the morning. We just put a single camera down and spun it around and cut the lights and got an extraordinary feeling. Rain, gale, and all. Finally, near the end, I suggested to Ryan Davies, the top Welsh TV star who played the Second Voice, that he ride the boar straight into the camera – which he did as we went scattering for our lives.

Yet everyone knows that you can't ride a boar. Or make a horse go backwards. But both happen in *Under Milk Wood*. Even the animals behave in that picture. The cows, the dogs, the children – everyone seemed to understand instinctively what we were about. There were none of the normal problems like wrangling with the extra's union. We were simply a part of an inspired, almost enchanted village life.

In short, it is an extremely irrational film. It is magical, it is like an incantation – you can just see it going over and over again, like the cycles of night to day, full moon to full moon, life to death and back again. It is, in its way, beyond sense: it is unreasonable. It is inevitable to wonder why it all came together this way. Those who are religious believe it is a great advantage to be serving something greater than yourself – in this case, the dead Dylan and his poetry in the place he was writing about. All I know with certainty is that I was making the film for one person – who is dead – and his widow came up to the after the first performance and said, "that is just what Dylan would have liked."

DISTRIBUTION? MY EYE

Under Milk Wood was selected in 1971 to open the Venice Film Festival. For in a crusade against elitism, no Golden Lion was to be awarded that year. And my film was the perfect compromise between stardom and village life. Quartered on the Lido, at the *première*, I found myself sat next to Gina Lollobrigida, who was wearing only ten thousand pearls over a skintight sheath. She stretched an arm behind my neck. "I hope you are divorced," she said. Fifty flashbulbs of the *paparazzi* flashed. In the morning, I had my Warhol moment of brief fame. I was Lollo's new toyboy of the week, though forgotten on the morrow by the next scandal, the showing of the shocking *The Devils*, with its cavorting naked nuns.

The president of the Festival was Réné Clair, and he paid me the greatest compliment of my life. "I wish I had made your film," he said. "*M'sieu*," I said, "I could not have made it without watching all your films." It was true. He was the master of that little bit of business in the background, so that there is always a chuckle or three coming from the audience. On the beach, I ran across Dustin Hoffman, who remembered not being big enough to play Sam Bennet, *alias* Dylan Thomas, in *Adventures In The Skin Trade*, and also his great definition in his part at the time in *Eh!*: "Satisfactory. Latin. Satis means enough. Factory. Enough bloody work."

After the opening of *The Devils*, in which Oliver Reed was literally beaten with iron bars and burned at the stake, I ran him down, too, under a striped awning. I was trying to make another film, called *Byron's Evil*; Oliver would play the poetic Lord and also Frankenstein from Mary Shelley's novel. Those hooded blue eyes were mesmerizing. He said he had never yet been to Venice, so I offered to take him in a speedboat from the Lido across the lagoon to view the city. With him came a young dumb blonde, who turned out to be wittier than Noel Coward and Marilyn

Monroe. As we approached the Grand Canal, she said, "I never knew Venice was on the water."

"Ah," I said gravely, "many people don't."

Then the exquisite Pat Kavanagh flew out to join me on the Lido, and who could prefer Lollo to her? Although we were never to stay together, she and Clare Peploe remained the regrets in my life. They both had the alluring quality of mystery in Italy, the hints of Botticelli and Bronzino and Leonardo da Vinci. May their memory always prevail, along with Dylan, my particular muse.

Bryan Forbes once said to me that what was done daily in film distribution would put anyone else in Sing Sing for ninety-nine years. To the lawyer belongs the spoils. Yet initially, I was the good boy of Wardour Street. From the wee budget of £300,000, I had returned £13,000 to the money. John Terry was aghast and amused.

"We have never at the Film Finance Corporation," he said, "had a producer who ever returned money to us. They have either stolen it or demanded more. You have also made an excellent film. So I am returning you £5,000 for your next project."

Most considerate. And I had very good reviews from Venice and the *première* in New York. Even Oscars were mentioned. But I had not the least idea what was really going on, chiefly through Jules Buck, who was in charge of selling the picture and selling me out. We had already had a row, when he tried to interfere to prove his power. As Executive Producer, he wanted to leave his mark on the picture before he stole it. When Willy Kemplen and I returned to cut the film in Wardour Street, Jules had demanded to see the rough cut and some of the rushes. That night, he rang me in a rage.

"Why did you shoot it that way? I can't effing cut it."

"That's why I shot it that way."

"I don't effing care if you're a six-foot clapper boy, I'll knock you down and cut that picture."

"You can't. It can only be cut one way. That's how it was shot. Like John Ford did. All shot straight from my head."

"It'll never effing work."

"Only my way, it will."

And it did. And Jules could do nothing about it. What he could do and did was beyond my ken for many long years. He formed a corporation in the Bahamas called Meadowfresh or Buttercup S.A. or some other sweet-smelling name to cover up the stench. His company took the over the world distribution of my film. Despite its excellent reviews in Europe and the United States, where the redoubtable Judith Crist called it 'a classic', *Under Milk Wood* was only sold to one country outside the British Commonwealth and the United States of America, and that was Spain. I met the gentlemanly distributor there, and he told me how he would like to die.

"A wonderful dinner," he said. "Lobster and champagne. And then a bit of business. And then make love to have a son. And then, gone."

Always, that little bit of business.

Until the late 'eighties, wherever I travelled in the world, I was told that *Under Milk Wood* had shown there, serially in Los Angeles on television, and in many other places including Hong Kong. Yet these frequent appearances were hardly ever shown on the occasional notices of returns, which I received. I should have remembered what Jules Buck had told me about Sam Spiegel, who never paid out O'Toole's share in *Lawrence of Arabia*.

"It was so simple. Sam just put the goddam cheques in a drawer and in another bank. And he forgot to mention them."

So did the cabal, which had made the necessary mistake of giving Timon Films the media copyright of *Under Milk Wood*. As all four of them have passed away, I can reveal the truth. To misquote H.L. Mencken's wise adaption of a Latin tag, *De Mortuis nil nisi bunkum* instead of *bonum*, I can only write, *De mortuis nil nisi bunko game*, a swindle by card-sharping. Or in this case, by tax fiddling and contract forging.

Seventeen years after I had made the film, Don Getz, an amiable film salesman who had married Buck's sister, told me why there were so few returns on *Under Milk Wood*.

"It wasn't distributed properly because Burton and Taylor and O'Toole each had a million dollars written off their taxes for making it. So the film had to make a maximum loss. But you had to have the copyright and not know. That made it clean."

In the profitable plot were Jules Buck and Hugh French, John Terry and David Higham, who would never have let such a seminal copyright go to me without a consideration. After another decade, I discovered worse. Higham had brought out a doctored contract without my signature, by which television rights in *Under Milk Wood* reverted to his agency after ten years. Law suits followed from me against the NFFC and the Higham agency. The most extraordinary deals for under-the-table money had been done. Even the British Film Institute was distributing my film – the claim was that it had been bought from a man in a bar in Pinewood Studios. After a flurry of threats and writs from me, I found an excellent and honest film distributor, Icon Entertainment, which sold *Under Milk Wood* to thirty countries, including Sundance and Universal Pictures. *Under Milk Wood* was recognized as a classic film at last and viewed across the world.

Yet such trickery was to have a remarkable legacy. The copyright in the major works of Dylan Thomas would be prolonged by Timon Films. In Europe, literary rights lasted for 70 years after the writer's death, and as early as 1953, the Welsh poet had died. And so, by 2023, his copyrights would expire. But I had made *Under Milk Wood* as a film in 1971, and its media rights extended to 2046 in Europe and to 2066 in the United States, where George W. Bush under extreme Hollywood and pop pressure had extended film and music rights to 95 years after they first came out. The situation was even more favourable with *Dylan on Dylan*, which I backed and made myself in 2002, on licence from the Higham agency with literary copyrights, which would expire after another 26 years. The screenplay was all in Dylan's own words and made with his daughter Aeron, who also played her mother. It comprised most of his second major autobiographical radio play, *Return Journey*, and seven of his major poems. Thus my film preserved these copyrights through most of the 21st century, also those of the 75 classic screenplays I had published in my Lorrimer heydays.

So what was I to do? By the quirk of movie law, the future of the Dylan Thomas heritage was passing to Timon Films outside the public domain. I had always been considered an infiltrator in Cardiff. For none but a Welshman could film *Under Milk Wood*, and even if I was a Celt of Scots and Irish descent, how could I understand? And so I began to seek some worthy heir, be it BBC (Wales) or London, for the wireless had made Dylan through his radio plays and talks in the Second World War. I was aged and death like dawn was inching up. Dylan was born in 1914 on the eve of the First World War. The centenary of his birth was not far away. Perhaps history and my long experience would solve the puzzle. As the great John Ford had said of making films: "There are no problems. There are only ways of doing it differently."

With the media rights in *Under Milk Wood* owned by my company Timon Films, and my end approaching after forty years of battling and guarding the Dylan gold like the dragon in *Beowulf*, I did not intend to die with the bardic hero and that awesome legacy. While my demise was finite, the screening and remaking of Dylan's classic work in the digital age was infinite. I knew I had to give back the greatest work of their great bard to the Welsh people, also to that Corporation which had broadcast his voice across the world. And so it was done.

I had been a professional historian of the United States, a Fellow of Cambridge and Columbia Universities, of Stanford and University College, London. On my way from Harvard to Hollywood, I had never found the right direction, so I used to say in Tinseltown that I was the only Don there not called Corleone. But I had also studied the Classics until I was seventeen years old, and then I had taught Political Philosophy to students from the London School of Economics – *Plato to Mao in ten easy lessons*. So from the example of our first democracy in Ancient Athens, I believed that if we were citizens, we had duties to the state as well as receiving rights from it. And from Immanuel Kant and the later Existentialists, I thought that we had moral duties, also that we would only be credited for our acts.

My duty was to return the rights of *Under Milk Wood* to the peoples of Wales through the Milkwood Trust, chiefly staffed by the best of BBC (Wales), which had acted for the Poet, when he was alive. On the Trust, for that it is, will serve Dylan's granddaughter, Hannah Ellis Thomas. May she be blessed in his memory.

For country and memory are all to me, in the end. And while *Under Milk Wood* begins in the beginning, the Welsh Trust is the ending of the end for me. For Dylan and myself, *requiescant in pace*.

Angharad Rees, dreaming of her wedding.

Teaching the wonderful children of Llareggyb.

Victor Spinetti and Glynis Johns, lying within their Valentine.

Dylan in the pub from *Return Journey*.

And death shall have no dominion.

Do not go gentle into that good night.

Aeronwy Thomas at the Boat House, Laugharne.

FINALE

Richard Burton had told me that *Under Milk Wood* had never left him. The Voices in that play sounded through his head a thousand times, awake or half-asleep. I never saw him or Elizabeth Taylor again, although I did bump into Peter O'Toole from time to time. He had wanted to play Gog, the lumbering hero of a mythological novel of mine. On the cover were the backs of my hands; I was tattooed in ink on one paw with the word *LOVE*; on the other, with *HATE*. "All those fights," he said to me at lunch. "I see you have broken knuckles, too." I saw little of him after that, except when sending up a portentous *Macbeth* and playing *Jeffrey Barnard is Unwell* to the Soho drunk born. Frail and austere, he came to the theatrical memorial tribute to his other Irish actor friend, Richard Harris. Both of them, Peter had told me, had lost their gizzard, their spleen and their lights, because of the gargle, and they had to give it up. "A lot of my plumbing," he said, "is gone." Harris, famously, when carried out of Claridge's *in extremis*, had shouted to the other guests, "It's the food."

Actually, it was the drink. At a memorial celebration in the Piccadilly Theatre, a Harris son described the effort of the Irish roisterers to survive. Before his end, Harris had emerged into Brook Street, to find O'Toole weaving along the pavement.

"O'Toole," Harris said, "look at you. Are we not new members of Alcoholics Anonymous?"

"Indeed," O'Toole said. "I am trying to find my way to the next meeting."

"But are you observing the rules?"

"It is very difficult," O'Toole agreed. "You see, every bar I enter, I have to give a false name."

What a lovely wit! Curiously enough, O'Toole remained religious, as only the irreverent can be. The medieval Mystery Plays seemed to him the basis of English drama. "It's fortunate for the Church," he told me, "that I chose the theatre." Even more fortunate, too, for the theatre was O'Toole's choice of it, to play there instead of in the pulpit.

Richard Burton had always wanted to be a writer, and a Dylanesque story of his, *A Child's Christmas in Wales*, was published. But as I heard, all his scribbling afternoons in Puerto Vallarta ended in crunched balls of paper after another bottle of vodka. A splendid and real writer, Edna O'Brien, did once upon a time declare herself a little bit insane and decided to give a New Year's Eve party – the coda to *Under Milk Wood*. The playwright Robert Bolt was there, speaking slowly after his stroke, phrasing each syllable, fearing intelligibility, and looking across to his reconciled ex-wife Sarah Miles for an interpretation, if that were needed. She had lately given up promiscuity for chastity and visions of God, and she now wore her hair in black Afro-braids.

Bolt coughed at me that he was doing a final screenplay, before working on another work for the stage.

"If – you – are – near – death – it – changes – you."

I suggested that the prospect of death not only concentrated the mind wonderfully, but also the vocabulary. Obviously, Robert now had to choose his words very carefully. He laughed and spoke slowly. Yes, each phrase mattered. He had been unable to find words, but now he felt them in him again. I then quoted Dylan Thomas, "The gift of the gab bangs back on the blind shaft," and I got off my knees and went to talk to Neil Kinnock who was ensnared by my bold and flashing stepdaughter Pandora, who had to dance aside.

Neil was bald with the tonsure of a monk. Only a red cowlick of side hair over his pink and freckled front pate hid the dome. He was talking of how the Animal Rights people in the Labour Party were losing votes. I said, "Three million anglers can't be wrong." He laughed and said, "We have a policy on fox-hunting, but not on bloody computers." In terms of wasted parliamentary time a quarter of a century on, what a prophecy!

We chatted for a long time on Wales and my film of *Under Milk Wood*. He had liked that, although not my added sexual bits. "Enough of that," Kinnock said, "already in Dullan's piece." He explained the early manhood of Richard Burton. Adoption was common at that time in poor Welsh families, and usually by schoolmasters. This was the way to get ahead by education. Rare, however, was to change your name. There must have been a special relationship between the young Richard Burton and his teacher, the older Philip Burton.

Kinnock then talked of getting dead drunk with his old father-in-law on Christmas Day on vodka, brought from Moscow. He told of beer marathons and faces being kicked in the pubs – "They put in the boot and the teeth went nuclear." These stories of a wild lost Welsh youth, as that of Richard Burton, showed that Neil lacked the bottom to lead the Labour Party or the country, in spite of his charm, his good heart, his great intelligence, and his working-class sympathies. In him, the gift of the gab banged back at you, ceaselessly.

Harold Pinter was there, his eyes owl-like and glittering behind his glasses. His wife Antonia, too, very matronly under a cap of blonde hair, saying that Harold didn't mind quarrelling with Peter Hall and leaving the National Theatre. Then she laid down the law:

"Writers are in very short supply. He doesn't have any trouble in getting his work placed."

The other writers there rather winced. Perhaps we weren't so talented, but – that sort of trouble was our daily business.

And so, to bed.

APPENDIX

I made the first film biography of the great Welsh bard, *Dylan on Dylan*, mainly in the poet's own words, with the help of the excellent Producer in Wales, Jeff Towns, now Chair of the Dylan Thomas Society of Great Britain alongside Dylan's grand-daughter Hannah Ellis Thomas. The final illustrations are from that film. As always, I shot my scenario to tell the story unless sad circumstances intervened, as the seals did in *UNDER MILK WOOD*. In this case, we had Dylan's daughter Aeronwy playing for us and the angel Angharad Rees, uniquely in both of my Dylan films, set against the brooding melancholy of Welsh cemeteries. They are both now gone, and this book mourns their grace and beauty, also the poet's undying ending.

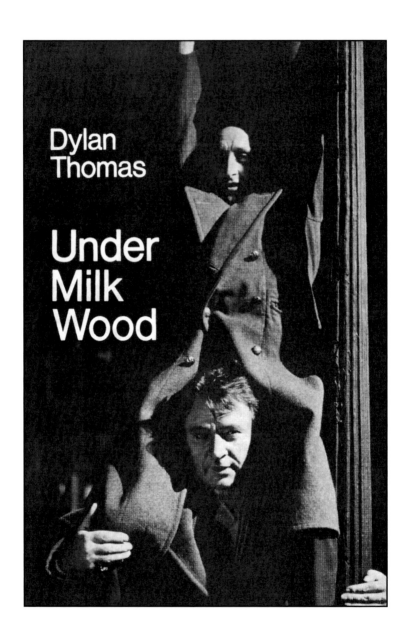

"**UNDER MILKWOOD** is a classic! I have seen the film three times; I shall see it at least three times more. Pure poetry!" —*JUDITH CRIST, New York Magazine*

"**UNDER MILK WOOD** seems like a miracle and a lovely one at that...perfect and unique!" —*BERNARD DREW, Gannett News Service*

"**UNDER MILK WOOD** is a glowingly beautiful film! Be sure—be absolutely sure—to see it!" —*GENE SHALIT, Ladies Home Journal*

"**UNDER MILK WOOD** is a beautiful, heady mixture of poetry and visual art. A concert for the eyes!" —*LOUISE SWEENEY, Christian Science Monitor*

"**UNDER MILK WOOD** is an accomplishment of considerable magnitude. O'Toole and Burton are almost awesomely fine." —*NORMA McLAIN STOOP, After Dark*

"**UNDER MILK WOOD** is a fascinating piece of work...lovely and dream like, a tone-poem of powerful moods and emotions." —*BOB SALMAGGI, Group W Network*

"**UNDER MILK WOOD** has an incandescent poetic intelligence that gleams through every line." —*BRUCE WILLIAMSON, Playboy*

JULES BUCK & HUGH FRENCH present AN ANDREW SINCLAIR FILM

RICHARD BURTON
ELIZABETH TAYLOR
PETER O'TOOLE
in DYLAN THOMAS'

UNDER MILK WOOD

SCREENPLAY AND DIRECTION ANDREW SINCLAIR GUEST STARS GLYNIS JOHNS · VIVIEN MERCHANT · SIAN PHILLIPS · JULES BUCK · HUGH FRENCH
MUSIC COMPOSED BY BRIAN GASCOIGNE · JOHN COMFORT · A TIMON FILMS PRODUCTION FILMED IN TECHNICOLOR · DISTRIBUTED BY ALTURA FILMS INTERNATIONAL [PG]

87

Screen adaptations of hard-to-slot items such as Dylan Thomas' "Under Milk Wood", completed just before the poet's death in 1953, have long been trying and tricky affairs, so it is a tribute to the makers of this pic that it's come off this well. At the box office, pic is basically special fare requiring personalized handling, but should find legs in the Richard Burton - Elizabeth Taylor - Peter O'Toole names as well as lasting values in other niches (college, educational, cassettes, etc,) and more obviously, as video fodder.

In addition to some stunning all-location photography to dress the scene, writer-director Andrew Sinclair has a wonderful feel for his material, and a happy hand in matching it to its setting. Normal screen conventions are broken as Sinclair chooses to follow Thomas instead in his dissection of a Welsh seaside village and its inhabitants, done with caustically keen and boisterously earthily humorous pen. As a result, actors (with the exception of O'Toole) impersonate more than perform, and a more colorful lot you've rarely seen.

O'Toole plays the blind but still all-seeing Captain Cat, with a (sometimes distracting) assist from makeup on the surface and a fine and oft-moving limn underneath. Burton is fully at ease in a physical walk-through of a village day, and he speaks the bulk of Thomas' voice-over lines with feeling and obvious love. Through him principally, the purr and the occasional soar of the poet's phrase flows and satisfies. Miss Taylor, glimpsed all too briefly, has rarely been more beautiful. A very distinguished roster of featured players, most playing telling cameos, completes the vast cast.

There are those who'll claim parts are long and repetitious and inevitably, some Thomas aficionados will have their own carps, but all factors considered, it's difficult job well done as well as an obvious labor of love involving physical and financial sacrifices on the part of most participants. Technically, as noted, pic's an outstanding achievement in all departments.

Hawk **VARIETY**

AND MORE GREAT CRITICS' QUOTES FROM ALL OVER

"The film, beautifully photographed and spoken, casts the brooding spell of Thomas' verse in its reconstruction of the seaside village and the daily round of its inhabitants."
THE INTL. HERALD TRIBUNE

"Meets its promises ... A delightful film .. Designed to excite even the world's most austere critics."
LA NOTTE

"A film with sincere inspiration and with humility."
IL TEMPO

"An impeccable act of fidelity ......a full-bodied, whimsical, glorious film."
IL GAZZETTINO

"A whole human microcosm, knowing and human, ferments in that village ... Memories, frustrated or hidden, innocence and brutality -- all these human sentiments express themselves in short sequences in which people live their actual lives or those of their dreams."
LE SOIR

"A touching experience and a true effort ..... we must pay homage to the great qualities of this film."
LE FIGARO

"Andrew Sinclair uses the eye of a painter ......Done with poetic beauty and also brutality, particularly in the smaller roles."
DIE WELT

"Poetry and prose, narrative and dramatic literature are beautifully blended in "Under Milk Wood" .....Gaiety and melancholy go arm in arm."
IL MESSAGERO